PEACE BY AFRICANS' PEACEFUL MEANS

RAÏS NEZA BONEZA

Protea Publishing

Peace By Afrcans' Peacefull Means
by Rais Neza Boneza

rais.boneza@eartharc.com

First Edition

ISBN 1-59344-098-7 soft cover

ISBN 1-59344-099-5 hard cover

USA Library of Congress Control Number: 2005920788

Protea Publishing (Imprint)
Las Vegas, Nevada, USA
southsky@earthlink.net
www.proteapublishing.com

I woke up in the domain of humans,
in the middle of the road,
between light and dreams of faith;
Africa must survive!
I said to myself.
My mind interfered
with far-melodic-remembrances
Of the civil right movement earlier in the sixties:

"We Shall Overcome…"

"A turning point has now been reached in Africa's history. After years of patient effort to achieve the total political and economic emancipation of the continent by peaceful means, only limited results have been achieved, and it has become essential to adopt a more militant and positive strategy. Kwame Nkrumah (14 June 1966) Foreword to Oginga Odinga "Not Yet Uhuru

"African Nationalism is meaningless, dangerous, anachronistic, if it is not at the same time pan-Africanism," Juluis Nyerere, late President of Tanzania.

"Many African leaders refuse to send their troops on peace keeping missions abroad because they probably need their armies to intimidate their own populations." Koffi Anon, UN secretary

"The greatest glory in living lies not in never falling, but in rising every time we fall."
-- Nelson Rolihlahla Mandela (b. 1918), Ex-President and South African political leader, jailed for anti-apartheid activities

"Peace is not merely a distant goal that we seek, but a means by which we arrive at that goal." Martin Luther King .Jr.

Chap. I. African Cosmologies

1. Ancient African Cosmologies
2. Contemporary Africa

Chap. II. Ethnic Relations Theory
Chap. III. Structural Violence in Africa
Chap. IV. Micro-cultural aspects of violence in Africa

* African Cultural Violence: Development and the Bantu/Nilotic myth

1. History of Virunga (Great Lakes Region)
2. Rising Nilo/Hamitic ideology
3. Afro-Hitlerism: Abatemu, Kulo-Kwor, Ynyenzi, Nteramwe

Chap.V. Macro-Cultural Aspect

1. Theory of colonization: "Diviser pour mieux Regner" in Africa
2. What Can we about it?

Chap.VI. Transcendental Culturology as Science of Cultural Peace

1. Kahalaria or Khoisan wisdom "Kgotla"
2. Baraza
3. Gacaca, Rwanda 97-2001
4. Kacoke Madit, Acholi (Uganda-North-sudan)

Chap VII. The Dark or Forgotten Continent?

Chap VIII. Path to a cultural democracy in Africa

Chap. IX. Final Conclusion: "Amani Na Salama" as a final draft of an African Culture of PEACE

Supplements

World citizen's democracy

A. Introduction
B. Different Styles of Democracy
C. Training for Democracy
D. Concept of Freedom
E. Conclusion

Overview on African Thought

1. Definition of the terms
    a. Philosophy in the strict sense
    b. Philosophy in general sense
    c. African Debate

2. The different trends in African philosophy
    a. Ethno philosophy
    b. The sage philosophy
    c. Professional Philosophy

3. The African's philosophy of universe

4. African Cosmogony
    a. African concept of times
    b. The Supreme Beings
    c. Notions of divinities
    d. The Spirits
    e. The Notion of the human

5. Positive inter-exchange between Africans and western thinkers

6. Political nationalistic philosophy or contemporary
   African philosophy

1. Nyerere Julius of Tanzania and Ujaama
2. Harambe of Jomo Kenyatta (Kamua)
3. Nyayo philosophy of Daniel Arap Moi
4.. Black consciousness philosophy of Steve Biko

ACKNOWLEDGEMENT

After almost six years in exile, I have shifted from a daily struggle for survival and liberty during my forced stay in different African countries, to a condition of fighting for education in a "welcoming" Scandinavian freedom. "La Lutta Continua"(1) as earlier African revolutionaries said.. The challenge today is about integration and education. I remember the first step while in exile and confined in a U.N. safe-house in Kampala for almost one and half years, I was without any means of information, only able to read rare old local newspapers in my limited space. There I felt that the Ugandan authorities, in connivance with local UNHCR's (United Nations High Commissioner for Refugees) workers, seemed to support a plan of censorship for those of us in safe houses, and refugees camps; in fact, they seemed to benefit from spoiling the refugees' chance to enrich themselves. After losing nearly three years of my life in forced hiding, I broke the rule with my thirst for learning and went outside to meet very nice men and women; I was soon given access to the Internet, and I was enrolled as poet in the crossing-border program initiated by the British High Counsel in Uganda, and later welcomed by Bruce Cook of AuthorMe.com (USA) . I was just a poet, dreaming about peace in a society mined by violence and abuse.

My arrival in Norway has brought me in contact with new friends and wonderful people. I choose to be part of the Peace and Art faculty of the TRANSCEND Peace University. In the meantime, while trying to establish myself in a new society, I am meditating, writing, researching; especially about non-violence and peace building, since I have chosen to dedicate my life to it. My dearest inspiration to promote peace comes from the TRANSCEND Art and Peace Network. From the philosopher Paulo Feire and the constructive analysis of Noam Chomsky, to the TRANSCEND Method of Johan Galtung; my inspiration has no limits. At the same time, my already strong feelings about Dr. Martin Luther King, Jr. have grown stronger. Today, the poet has transcended identities and mere ideologies to be just a "menneskelige borger" (From Norwegian: human citizen).

My first dedication goes to Prof. Johan Galtung for his dedication to world peace and Non-violence. My highest reconnaissance to President Ikeda of the Soka Gakkai International.   Dr. Marisa Anatoya of the Peacelit/ University of Science and Technology in Chonburi (Thailand) for your friendship, assistance and patience. Prof George Kent University of Hawaii, Vegar Vjorlanger Building Peaces/Norwegian University of Science and technology, Bernt Hauge and The Trondheim Menneskerettighethus (Norway), Prof. Boneza Rumvegeri of the Geological Survey of Norway, María Elena López Vinader From Argentina/Music Therapist, Prof. Olivier Urbain Sokka University, Theresa Wolfwood of The Barnard-Boecker Centre Foundation, (BBCF) a peace and social justice foundation in Victoria,BC, CANADA, The Transcend Peace University (TPU), The Transcend Art and Peace Network, Building Peaces.

Thanks for the The Norwegian Non-Fiction Writers and Translators Association (NFF) by supporting my research and promoting the right to free expression.

INTRODUCTION

HUMANISM OR PRE-TRANSCEND PERIOD

Humankind seems to have cultivated for thousands of decades an uncontrolled thirst for violence. However, human needs, whatever their background, are similar; we constantly seek peace while the drums of war beat strongly in many parts of the planet.

The deep human nature is to compete, dominate, and control, and these are the natural predecessors to aggressiveness and violence. On the other hand, the Augustinian tradition of peace, synthesised as "Tranquilitas Ordinis", reflects immobility, silence, kindness, wisdom, and stagnation. Tranquilitas ordinis means that Peace is not merely the absence of war, but the preservation of the right order by all means.

However, Tranquilitas Ordinis also tries to defend the theory of a just war. St. Augustine argues in the City of God that "Pacifism may be a desirable and, in certain circumstances, a compelling individual response to violence or the threat of violence, but it cannot suffice as the governing moral criterion for a magistrate, who owes a duty in charity and justice to his subjects to protect them against the designs of evil men" (5)The Tranquilitas Ordinis is therefore a theory that defends the Just-violence or the Just-war. Today, major states are still inspired by the Just-war ideology that labelled others adversaries to be evil, outlaw nations.

Peace may be impossible in an imperfect where men and women are conscious of their direct connection with their environement. Actually, in the four Kingdoms (animal, vegetable, mineral, and human) that compose our nature, only one element troubles the harmony of the others: The human kingdom. War, environmental extinction and other catastrophes are produced by humans.

13

The promotion of a new global order promoted by superpowers shows that peace can never simply mean a state of tranquility. Those superpowers that try to exercise unchecked power in the global arena tend to grow up and become evil empires themselves. This confirms that seeking tranquillity in peacetime may be unrealistic, although tranquility is certainly an essential component of peace. To assume that conflict should be avoided is purely a utopia or an evasion from social reality. The wrong idea of peace that has been globalized and imposed by certain powers is rooted in the foundation of a self-definition of "ends and means."

This work is a meditation on the probable source of conflicts in Africa and their effect on humanity, particularly on Africans.

TRADITIONS OF CONFLICT RESOLUTION

In African traditions, exalting heroes and warriors is a common cultural characteristics. The exploits of Shaka (Zulu), Sundiata Keita (Mali), Lianja (Great-Lakes) are often praised.

The Just War School is a group of thinkers who support the idea of a world of perpetual confrontations as healthy for human revolution. Heraclites said "war was the father and the king of everything." (7) In the same vein, Hegel asserted that "war is the motor in the progress of Humanity." Until now, the church and many other religions have sustained the thesis of a "Holy War" as acceptable. There are, again, more extreme theories, such as "The wish of power" theory of Friedrich Nietzsche or the "exalted militarism" of Heinrich Von Treitschke. According to the writer Friedrich Von Bernhardi, war is a unique way for 'civilized nations' to manifest their superiority and vitality, and he favours an emphasis on better human values.

Another type of thinking about peace is pacifism, which presupposes that violence is always and everywhere wrong. In a practical sense, it is usually manifested as an opposition to war and other forms of state-sanctioned violence against people. In the early period of Stoicism, or in Christianity before the church developed into a militarist power, non-violence was usually preached and promoted. But while religion played this role in traditional society, the doctrine of peace (and peace research), later was advanced, structured, and promoted by intellectuals and artists.

J.J.Rousseau proposed the creation of European states which would ensure the stability of all the European countries. (8) Kent presented a similar solution in: "Zum Ewingen Frieden" (9). Kent explored ways to eliminate the causes of war and create friendly relations between nations.

Johan Galtung's method asserts that peace is always associated with harmony. Everything in creation is in a state of harmony, except human beings. Human Beings are inherently in a state of disharmony with different aspects of themselves. This new tradition explores the problematic from the human level to the macro/micro level, best rooted in non-violence. People like Martin Luther King, Jr, (USA), the Dalai Lama, Nelson Mandela (South Africa), or Dr. Ikeda are the mentors of the non-violence movement. Inspired by the non-violence movement, Johan Galtung develops the TRANSCEND method as a new dimension in dealing with conflicts. He defines peace as "The capacity to handle conflicts with creativity, non-violence and empathy."

The Transcend Method presents new approaches regarding the resolution of conflicts. It does so more realistically, since, according to the TRANSCEND method, we must accept that conflict exists and cannot be avoided.

I will explore some dimensions in the development of conflict:

a. Conflict can be constructive when it gives us the opportunity to create new solutions to problems, to learn about ourselves and become closer to each other.

b. However, conflict can be destructive when it harms one or both parties. When we are talking about conflict, we must avoid including violence directly in the picture. Violence is the external expression of conflict. And in all cases, violence is destructive, hurting one or both parties.

c. Conflicts can exist at the inter-personal level; for example, between friends. Conflict can also exist within communities or at the international level.

d. Conflicts can involve a number of interconnected or intertwined levels: a conflict between friends can also involve a conflict between families, between political or cultural differences, and even between nations.

The mainstream in avoiding open cruelty and prior violence is our capacity to handle creatively a situation of crisis before it becomes a catastrophe. Then, the conflict becomes constructive because the relationship between both parties improves, and the atmosphere is comfortable.

TOWARD PEACE

The TRANSCEND method does not only focus on the simplistic method of "le retour a l'ordre etablit," following the centurial "Tranquilitas Ordinis" of Augustinian tradition, (see Different traditions of conflict resolution) or the famous Roman dictum: "Si vis pacem, para bellum" (TRANSLATE!) that has been applied by most of the states and powers for almost 2000 years. Rather, through the TRANSCEND method we develop the capacity to transform conflicts constructively and without violence.

Violence is here defined as the cause of the difference between the potential and the actual (See Galtung J. 1969). Violence ...when human beings are influenced so that their actual somatic and mental realizations are below their potential realizations."

Peace studies are about creatively resolving conflicts and calling the parties involved to see the conflict itself as creatively challenging; to focus on underlying needs instead of positions; to use non-violent techniques whenever possible, considering and knowing that violence is unethical and ineffective as it is described in the TRANSCEND Method.

This work is a meditation on the probable source of conflicts in Africa and their effect on humanity, particularly on Africans. Through structural research on violence, we shall explore and comprehend the conception of conflict in Africa, its cultural roots, its development and its current psychological and physical consequences on African societies.

First, consider the wisdom of the Shi's (an ethnic group from East-DR Congo) which classifies the structural source of violence as follows:

- The U-Mugoshe aspect (Violation or immorality)

Shi' people consider U-mugoshe as resulting from a violation of U-muziro. U-mugoshe is compatible with the meticulous calculation of self-interests, a constant evaluation of actions for which the truth is meaningless, giving way to egocentrism, barbarism, crimes, and the spreading of lies. Those are t tht he aspects which justify the notion of "the means justifies the end, corresponding to the depraved morality that constitutes more than anything else the syndrome of cultural violence in Africa.

- The U-Muziro aspect (Taboo or non-violation)

U-Muziro corresponds to the morality concept of Ubuntu (from the Sub-Saharan region), that is the undisputable sublime side of the African culture in general and implies the respect of human dignity, the nobility of the heart, goodness and wisdom, responsibility, respect for one's own person and for others. Umuziro is the stronghold of a culture of peace in Africa. It is the equivalent of Ubuntu, an African term meaning "humanity towards others." The Zulu version can be found in the sentence "Umuntu ngumuntu ngabantu" translated as "a person becomes a person through other persons" (Ramose, 1999:49f; Shutte, 1993:46)

Violence   ...when human beings are influenced so that their actual somatic and mental realizations are below their potential realizations."

This work explores the TRANSCEND Method as it applies to Sub-Saharan Africa: cosmology, ethnic relations, cultural violence, colonization, and cultural peace. It offers a challenge, suggesting a path to cultural democracy and the "Amani Na Salama" as a final draft of an African Culture of PEACE

CHAPTER I

AFRICAN CULTURAL COSMOLOGIES

Culture is conceived as the main symbol of the human condition; it might be defined as a collective subconscious, described by the beliefs, behavior, language, and entire way of life of a particular group of people at a particular time. Culture includes customs and ceremonies; and also works of art, inventions, technology, and traditions.

By cultural cosmology, we understand the study of the culture as a whole; this includes theory about its genesis and evolution and in addition its general structure and future. It includes the collectively held subconscious ideas about what comprises normal and natural reality (Johan Galtung, Peace by Peaceful means 1996; page 211). Therefore, to better understand the different facets of cultural violence in Africa it is important to explore the cultural cosmology of Africa. That will allow us to understand the sources of early, traditional or contemporary violence in African societies.

Johan Galtung (10) described the six major cosmologies of civilization as:

* Occident I and Occident II, which are a mixture of the three Abrahamic religions: Judaism, Christianity, and Islam. Occident I is modern and in expansion, whereas Occident II is medieval and in contraction.

* Indic (Hindu)
* Buddhic (Buddhist)
* Sinic (Chinese)
* Nipponic (Japanese)

Our concern it is to demonstrate the link or influences of the previous cosmological classification on the African Cosmology.

19

Africa is composed of 51 independent countries today, and it is inhabited by two major groups: The "Caucasoid", in North Africa, Egypt and Sudan, with brown eyes, light olive skin, and high-bridged narrow noses. The "Black", in the rest of Africa are subdivided into numerous tribes and races. The Pygmies in tropical central Africa are one of the shortest people in the world. In tropical Africa alone, some 1,000 different languages are spoken. In each language group there are different tribes and religious denominations. Arabic is predominant in northern Africa. Berber is also spoken in northern Africa. Bantu languages are spoken throughout central and eastern Africa. Sudanic is spoken in the large grassland region south of the Sahara. Hausa is spoken in western Africa and many countries, after their independence, kept as official languages one of the European languages: French, English, Portuguese, Spanish, German, Dutch (e.g. Afrikaans, derived from German)....

Egyptian cosmology as a primary African Cosmology:

The African cosmologies are linked to ancient Egypt. The diverse ethnic elements and alien influences of the macro-cultural aspects make it too complex to classify a unified African cosmology.

Considering the movement of evolution in the African cosmogony, the eternal created matter passes from one stage to another until it becomes conscious of itself. In this way, the first consciousness springs up from Nous in Egyptian thoughts. The Greek word Nous means God. The Egyptian demiurge Ra, who brings creation to completion, created four divine couples:

- Geb and Nut unite with Ra to create the earth and skies
- Shou and Tetnout unite with Ra to create the air and space
- Osiris and Isis unite with Ra who also unit with Ra to create human beings, called Adam and Eve
- Seth and Neth unite with Ra to create Evil.

We can conclude that with the conception of Ra, an idealistic or spiritual element appeared in Egyptian cosmogony. Later, this idealistic element influenced the Greek philosophers and became the basis of Greek idealism. Ra is the first God; he has neither father nor mother, He is auto-genus, and not engendered.

Most people ignore the fact that ancient Nubia was the site of an early advanced black African civilization that rivaled ancient Egypt in wealth, power, and cultural development. For nearly one century, N Nubian kings ruled over Egypt as pharaohs. (Mellom 1970) In 1520 B.C., the Egyptian pharaohs took over, and Egyptian culture increasingly influenced Nubia. In the 11th century B.C., Nubia regained its independence and a new Nubian kingdom, based in Jebel Barkal in Napata, adopted an Egyptian model of the monarchy, including royal brother-sister marriages. In 742 B.C. Pianshi, king of Napata, conquered Egypt and founded the 25th Dynasty, which ruled Egypt for nearly a century. Soon after the conquest, the Nubian capital shifted to Meroë. The Meroë kingdom developed its own form of writing as well as an iron-based industry.

NEGROID COSMOLOGY

In the black African cosmogony, the idea of "vital force" dominates ideas. We understand that the vital force can be found in person or spirits; in persons, spirits, kings, chiefs, and mysterious persons that continue the perpetuation of God's work. Besides the current cohabitation of the Occident I and II, imposed by colonialism, there is a minor aspect of the traditional religion that still persists and in most cases, has been incorporated in those other religions: Animism.

Animism derives from the Latin word "anima" meaning breath or soul. its origin could be dated to the Paleolithic age. On it earlier belief, it suggested that a soul every object, even inanimate has a soul. In anthropology, animism is considered as to be the original human religion, being defined simply as belief in the existence of spiritual beings. African "primitive religions" are based on nature worship, and may have in common three types of occultism: Divination, witchcraft (magic) and spiritism, with the "sacrifice" of animals, and sometimes of humans, to calm the gods-demons; and reverence for the "ancestors." Often, the head of the tribe, or the Mwami or Pharaoh, is the "god."

As in the Zulu example, in Africa there are generally two kinds of diviners: The isangoma is a medium who can make contact with the ancestors. And the isanus, is a diviner capable of "smelling out" sorceresses and other evil-doers. The herbalists, inyanga yokewlapha, still have the task today of administering medicines made from plants and animals.

The Muslims in the North, and the Christians in the South of the Sahara Desert, have changed most of African religion, but it is estimated that more than 40% of Africans still practice "animism", often in syncretism with their new Christian or Muslim religions. The "Maraboutism" (11) in west-Africa is proof of the influence of the traditional on imported religion. (Rais – explain how these influences worked, briefly.) We can observe that the forces of Christianity and Islam are often seen as clashing. In Africa, these two religions competed for the soul of a continent, and they have enhanced the beginning of globalization with all its consequences on the African style of life. The movement can be observed as a transposition of the Occident I and II cosmologies (12) on the African cosmology. Therefore, contemporary Africa is divided into four major alien cosmologies: Occident I and Occident II, Islam separately and Animism.

a.3. Contemporary Africa

Tab.a.3.1. Four implanted cosmologies

occident I	occident II	African-Islam	Animism

Autochthones: Proto-Bantu and Bantu	Nilo-hamitic	Sudano-Nilotic-Arab	Traditional in general
Major part of the Sub-Saharan Africa	In the horn of Africa: Ethiopia, and Eritrea, Egyptian Coptic Church	**The Horn of Africa:** Somalia, Sudan, Djibouti are the Principal poles. **West Africa** (Neo-Sudanese States): Mali, Ghana, Nigeria… **North of Africa**	A relic of the ancient traditional African religion. Expressed under different rites according to geo-political influences. Therefore, it can be traditional or be mixed with new religions such as Islam, Christianity and others.

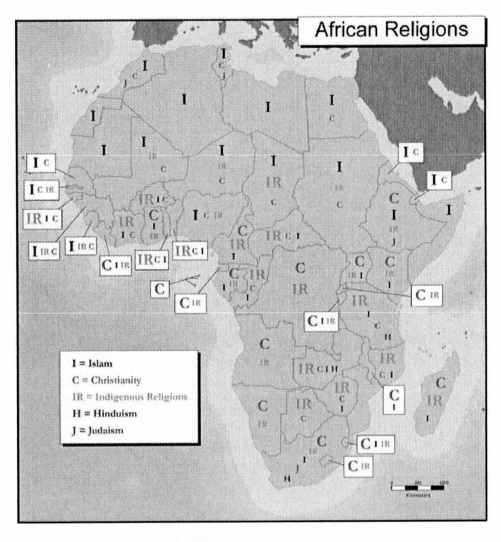

Tab 3.2 African imposed religion, source exploring Africa (Michigan Universisty, African Study Departement)

a.4. Four cosmologies expressed in seven spaces

Human creations are first thoughts before they become physical. The creations of communities with a structural organization such as cities within an administration with achievements such as art, sciences and technologies— things that make a civilization — must spring from thought. In Johan Gultan's TRANSCEND method, cosmology is to a civilization what the personality is to a person (13).Thus a socio-cultural code which is a set of structural rules for survival and success that a particular group of people has developed; it provides an individual with roles, telling Her/him who to be, how to act, what is correct to say and to whom.

The hybridization of African culture has affected the local and cultural values both negatively and positively, especially because of the added alien technology, economy, and supremacy of colonization.

To compare the Indic or Buddhist ways with the African cosmology is to find some similarities in the meaning of visions about life and the environment. African cosmology has contributed to the origin of what has been described in Galtung's book as Occident I and Occident II, a mixture of the three Abrahamic religions: Judaism, Christianity and Islam. It is widely agreed among secular historians that the first absolute monotheist in recorded history was an African – Pharaoh Akhenaton of Egypt of the 18th Dynasty (1379-1362 BCE).

If monotheism is considered as a concept, the most globalized religious doctrine, the most influential monotheistic religions have been Judaism, Christianity, and Islam. Africa played a part in the origins of all these three religions. All of them started with Semitic peoples. Scholars do not know whether Semitic peoples originate in Africa or in Asia? Today, Semitic languages are on both sides of the Red Sea. Amharic and Tigrinya are among the "Black Semitic languages.

Is it possible that Moses was an Egyptian and therefore an

African? Writers and thinkers like Sigmund Freud have argued that Moses, founding father of Judaism, was an Egyptian. Did Jesus Christ find asylum in ancient Egypt when King Herod threatened his family with death? The Gospel according to Matthew tells us so (Mathew Chapter 2, Verses 13 to 23). Did the first Arabicized Muslims find asylum in Ethiopia after the Hijra?

Western technology and economic structure were introduced with the help of a completed External religion (Christianity) that has contributed most to the alienation and the loss of identity and the division of Africans. This is because the subversion resulting from hybridisation has created a "murderous identity. Those external influences have affected African societies, creating and hybridising their culture and providing a new type of horrifying and hopeless cultural violence. Violence in the name of ethnicity or beliefs in Africa and the Third World is a direct result of Humiliation (See In the Name of Identity: Violence and the Need to Belong, By Amin Maalouf, 1996). If we want to address the problem of ethnically or religiously motivated violence, we must work to counter the conditions under which people are humiliated or denigrated for being part of an ethnic, religious or national group.

Tab a.4.1. Galtung's seven spaces relating to African Contemporary Cosmologies.

Alien Cosmologies: Occident I	Occident II	Islam	New-Animism

Autochthone: Proto-Bantu and Bantu states	Nilotic hamitic states	Sudano-Nilotic-Arab states	Generally represented in both states

The Seven Spaces (See Peace by Peaceful means 1996, page 213)

Nature: humans over nature, Herrschaft, Meatism	Humans over nature, Life over non-life, Herrschaft Mixed	Humans over nature, Herrschaft, meatism	Humans and sentiment, life over non life, herrschaft, mixed
Self: weak, mixed ego, Weak Identity	Strong, super-ego, strong identity	Strong Ego, Super Ego, strong identity	Strong ego, mixed ego, weak identity
Society: ethnic and gender, collective,	Ethnic, class and gender, collective	Ethnic, gender, collective	Ethnic, class, gender, collective....
World: Bounded	Each part a center, umbounded	Each part a center, umbounded	One center, bounded
Time: Emotionally generally umbounded	Bounded	bounded	Unbounded
Transpersonal: imminent one Gods many gods Devils one soul *(Ntu)* people *(Bantu)* eternal malediction(Umugoshe) Reward mixed, plur/univ.	Transcendant and imminent, one God one Satan one soul people eternal One Hell Heaven Sing/Univ	Transc. Imminent one God one Satan one soul people Eternal One Hell Heaven Sing/Univ.	Transc. Imminent Many Gods One Satan One soul People Eternal Hell Plur./univer.
Episteme: Holistic Contradiction	Holistic Deductive No contradiction	Holistic Deductive No contradiction	Holistic Eclectic No contradiction

CHAPTER II

ETHNIC RELATIONS THEORY

Africa is a composite of fragmented multi-ethnic nation-states. Virtually every African belongs to a "tribe" or ethnic group and there is nothing fundamentally wrong with belonging to one. On the whole, there is not a universal African identity or an essence of Pan-Africanism.

During the colonial period, Africa's colonizers frequently favored some groups and exploited tensions among others as a method of securing and maintaining power (See Diviser pour mieux Regner). After gaining independence, many African states have had to face the challenge of reconciling a multi-ethnic population. As is the case all over the world, establishing stability and peace and unity within its multi-ethnic nation-states has been a major challenge for the continent.

Many Africans identify themselves much more naturally by their ethnic groups than with their nation-states. This is due to the fact that when Europeans colonized Africa they created borders without regard to the interests or customs of diverse ethnic groups. Some borders divided people belonging to the same ethnic group and others brought together groups that had always lived separately. In many cases, rival groups were expected to work together under newly created national governments.

Overview of the Great-Lakes region

The Great-lakes region of Africa has been devastated by years of violence. The war has been perpetrated in the region has claimed more than 4 million victims. Under a succession of hegemonic and dynastic look-like systems of governance, the most human rights structures are destroyed in these societies. The rising of ethnic extremists and warlords against each other and their civilian hostages – The proliferation of small arms and light weapons (SALW) has acted to increase conflicts in

28

Burundi, Rwanda, and Democratic Republic of the Congo (DRC), Sudan, Angola, and Congo-Brazzaville, Uganda and in the entire region. The most serious impact of the conflict is the plight of populations subjected to lamentable crime against humanity, from mass killings to mass rapes, ethnic slaughter to forced starvation, and legalisation of child soldiering.

This analysis is an attempt to creatively discuss different alternatives in the process of building peace through Reconciliation, Reconstruction, and Resolution of cyclic Great-lakes conflict. It will be developed through a comprehensive deduction of structural elements that spawn conflict, the actors who seek geopolitical interests, and the structures that plays a strategic role in designing untransformed conflict designing the region.

1. Description of the situation since the 1990's

In Democratic Republic of Congo, Laurent Desire Kabila, leader of the Rally of Democratic Forces for the Liberation of Congo (AFDL), backed by Rwandan and Ugandan forces, took over the power in Kinshasa in May 1997, forcing the Mobutu and members of his regime into exile. Once an auto-proclaimed head of state, Laurent Desire Kabila tries to get rid of his former allies. Kigali is convinced and accuse him of connivance with FAR (former Rwandan Army) and Interamwe militias who participated in the Rwandan genocide in 1994.

The new development between Kigali and Kinshasa will drives the Rwanda and Uganda forces to support different Congolese rebels groups. The advance the rebel groups will be stopped only by the military intervention of Angola, Zimbabwe, Namibia and Chad support to the Kabila's regime. This conflict, considered as the first African continental war, will do almost 4 millions of victims. Six official foreign armies and about twenty armed movements will wage war, principally in East of the Congo. January 16 2001, Laurent Desire Kabila is murdered. His son, Joseph Kabila, providentially takes his succession.

After accessing to power, Kabila's son proclaims his willingness to apply the Lusaka in 1999 ceasefire agreement signed by the principal rebel movement; the MLC (Movement of the Liberation of Congo) and the two tendencies of the RCD (Congolese Rally for the Democracy); and between Kinshasa and its allies (Zimbabwe, Angola and Namibia) and Uganda and the Rwanda. The moderation of Joseph Kabila allows the relaunching of the cooperation with the international community for the reconstruction and peace settlement in the country.

The UN Security Council deployed UN liaison personnel in August 1999 to support the ceasefire. The liaison office became the UN Organization Mission in the Democratic Republic of Congo (MONUC) in November 1999, and in February 2000 it expanded in mandate and personnel. With an area the size of Western Europe, covered by dense tropical forest, the DRC poses a great challenge to the UN.

In November 2003 the Pretoria agreement between the transitional government of Burundi and Armed groups from the CNDD-FDD (the coalition forces for the defence of democracy). In Rwanda, the country under the Trauma of the 1994 genocide still on it long lasting way toward democracy and peace; has various political forces and Rebel groups specially the FDLR still demanding a forum of Dialogue and political freedom

The Burundian civil war lasts since 1993, with more than 300 000 victims, essentially civilian populations. The conflict opposes the majority Hutu (85% population) to the Tutsis, who hold the power. The first peace dialogue took place in 1998. In 2000, the principal protagonists, in the exception of the two principal movements rebel – the FDD (Forces for the Defence of Democracy) and the FNL (National Forces of Liberation) – sign to Arusha a peace agreement that foresees a division of the strength between Hutus and Tutsis. Nevertheless, the war continues. In April 30 2003, the vice president, Domitien Ndayizeye, a Hutu, succeed the president Buyoya for the 18 last months deal of the transition.

Although a light of hope so far has arisen from the passivity of the international community regarding the Great-lakes conflict. The Great-lakes region still instable as the presence of rebels movement, different militias along the borders bring tension and prediction of a regain of atrocities

2. Conflict Diagnosis

The conflict of the Great Lakes results in several factors, which can be dated between post-colonial, colonial and pre-colonial period. The structural sources will refers to static social, physical, and economic factors that either limit or spread conflict and shape dramatic responses practices among the actors.

a. Irrational Boundaries: In pre-colonial, the European-designed country in the Great-Lakes region did not exist as it is nowadays. The Virunga region is a land of high mountains, rich watered, free of malaria, a domain of volcanoes. From their arrival, The Europeans viewed the Great Lakes Region, as well as Africa in general, as a *terra nullius*. Although the region was composed to quite sophisticated societies, in some cases even with fairly well developed forms of governance—even though most were not European-style state structures.

The new delimitation that had served only German, Belgian and later England interest engendered a modern Rwanda and Burundi with little wealth and relying only on their fertile land. The richest mineral deposits were left to the Dem. Rep.of the Congo side of the border. Tens of thousands of Rwandophile reside along the Rwanda/Uganda boundary because of the British-negotiated 1910 cession of the Kisoro sub-district to Uganda. Often Tutsi and Hutu (Rwandophile) located on the other side of the Rwanda or Ugandan borders trace their ancestry to eastern Congo-North-Kivu province. Others members of the same Ethnical background were brought to migrate a bit deeper in the Dem.Rep.Congo following the new demarcation or for workers supply in the region.

The condition of the divided population living around the borders of states has helped fuel mutual destabilisation between neighbouring countries. For example in 1996, the uprising of a balkanisation tendencies that accentuated discourses to the expulsion of Rwandophile populations despite their centurial-old ancestry in the Kivu; triggered cyclic violence that resulted in a generalization of ethnical violence in the region. *Nåtildags*, The conflict ethnical background in the Great-Lakes today is tied to a unfair competitive gaining land whether by territorial expansion, genocide, or expelling certain ethnic groups.

In conclusion, the Great Lakes region has a long dated deep culture of hatred due to previous unfair systems that elevated one group and disadvantaged the other. The challenge in building peace will be to create mechanism that would allow healthy relationship based on equalitarian and democratic practices.

B. Actors in The conflicts: A similar particularity in the Great Lakes demonstrated that the power in those countries is based on structural antagonism between groups. One group has repressed another so the right to revenge is non negotiable. The actors can be subdivided as: 1. Direct Actors (In R.D.Congo, Uganda, Sudan, Tanzania, Rwanda and Burundi) 2. Extra-regional actors (mostly country in the western hemisphere and their agencies).

B.1.Direct actors: Two case are presented here:

-        **The Zaïrian Case or the Mobutism (D.R.Congo)**: The Late President Mobutu dominated for 30 years Zairian politics since the United States orchestrated the overthrow of the elected Prime Minister Patrice Lumumba in 1960 who was assassinated later, The United States opposed Lumumba's nationalist and non aligned policies, considering him as an extension of the Soviet Union's foreign policy. Since the 1965 coup d'etat Mobutu has been among the most autocratic, repressive, and corrupt dictators in the Third World. Mobutu reshaped the Democratic Republic of The Congo in his own image, rename it Zaïre, Initiate the politic of authenticity. Mobutu was widely thought to be using ethnic conflict in both Katanga (South-Congo) and Kivu (East-Congo) to his advantage and possibly even to be encouraging the fighting. He feudalised the army by creating new unit commanded by his family clan or his related regional tribe of the Equatorial region (North-Congo). He travelled to Goma in the Kivu in July 1993 promising equal rights to the Rwandophile speaking population But, there were reports that Mobutu's military had provided weapons to both sides in the conflict and had taken part in the looting and killing. Under his reign, the country was decadent mined by tribalism, favouritism and nepotism clanic at all level of the state. This situation created a contre-reaction that fuelled clashes between army units, tribes, provinces, and neighbouring states. Mass refugee movements from Burundi/Rwanda into The Congo from 1993 through 1996 further destabilised its eastern border area and set off a civil war that would lead to the collapse of the Mobutu regime and bring its army into full-scale war with neighbouring states.

-        **The Ugandan Case and The Fall of the Northerner**: After fifteen years of civil war, the National Resistance Movement came to power in 1986 leaded by the currently President Yoweri Kaguta Museveni. In his essay, "Uganda Since Impedance" (1992); P.Mutibwa said: The *conflict in Northern Uganda is fuelled by ethnic*

32

underpinnings that were exacerbated by colonial rule and were later to be manipulated by the post-independence administrations. During the colonial era the Ugandan society was largely divided between the North and the South and the North as opposed to the South, was sub-divided between the Acholi, Langi and the West Nilers. It has been observed that the fact the NRM (National Resistance Movement), an organization mostly of Southerners, produced new cleavages that have yet to be overcome and are manifested clearly in the armed struggle. He added: *The key role of the military in politics and of ethnic competition became evident under the first government of Milton Obote, who used the army to overthrow the constitution and the king of Buganda, a region from which the constitutional monarchy originated. Obote's use of the military led to his overthrow by Idi Amin, who was himself toppled by the Uganda Liberation Front/ Army (UNFL/A), assisted by the Tanzanian army in 1978. The brief presidencies of Yusuf Lule and Godfrey Binaisa followed, while a military commission held real power.*

B.2. Extra-Regional Actors

Extra-regional actors are those from outside the conflict area seeking to either ameliorate or exploit the conditions of war. The antagonism raised by the struggle between Anglo-Saxon and the Francophile in Africa, has contributed to the marginalisation by the international communities of the priority of the Africans, which remains the instauration of the democracy. The transcend perspectives has observes, that:

"The projection of the European (Anglo-French) tribal feud over linguistic/cultural/economic influence in Africa.

Uganda/Tutsi/Bunyamelenge/Kabila anglophiles are pitted against Hutu/Mobutu Francophiles, with the Western media traditionally dominated by the French as "area specialists". But disasters tend to favour the spread of English as most disasters are managed in English. French/Roman Law is losing ground, it seems, and English/Common Law is pushing westward with energy. (*See www.transcend.org)"*

After the end of the cold war, western policy toward Africa has changed by promoting fast calqued manufactured democracies in Africa. It has resulted in enflaming sleeping immature cells of oppositions in former

33

dictatorial regime, which created circles of instability throughout the continent.

The government of the United States is concerned about instability in D.R.Congo has it is aligned with Uganda and Rwanda. The Americans use Uganda for their effort to against the insurgence of Islamism (Sudan, Somali). This includes necessary funds and logistic for forces seeking to overthrow Sudan from bases inside Uganda, Eritrea, and Ethiopia. American Special Forces have also been assigned to train the RPF in counter-insurgency techniques. The American support has increased since the Bush war on Terror countries such Kenya and Tanzania are favourite beneficiaries.

France was aligned with Dem. Rep. of the Congo and Former Rwanda government. From 1990 to 1993 elite French forces along with the Mobutus' army backed Rwanda's government against the RPF (Rwandan Patriotic Front) leaded President Kagame. They also tried to intervene in 1994 to prevent further RPF attacks on the Hutu dominated government. A key issue of western powers (French and Anglo-Saxon influence) is the access to the vast natural and strategic wealth of the Congo curvet. The Dem. Rep. of the Congo's natural wealth and the attraction between arms dealers and war has seen a rapid proliferation of extra-regional involvement. Surplus arms including have come from former Yugoslavia to reach all sides at bargain prices [Ashworth 1996; Misser 1996]. Illegal operators and security firms in Britain and South Africa have also provided arms and mercenaries [Boggan 1996].

3. Prognosis

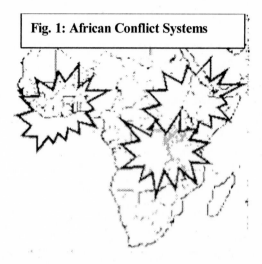

Fig. 1: African Conflict Systems

The Great Lakes conflict function in a system of *"vases communicant" (Matrix)*. Conflicts can start from one epicenter and be propagated to another. As Bethuel Kiplagat stated at Africa is presently host to three, partly overlapping conflict systems: In West Africa with the epicentre presently in Sierra Leone, but previously in Liberia; in the Horn of Africa with the epicentre presently in Sudan; and in the Great Lakes Region where the epicentre was previously in Rwanda but presently in the DRC (See Fig. 1).

The conflict in Sub-Saharan countries is not a simple fight for power, as would be the case between two opposed political parties or a simple fight between tribes or ethnic groups; rather, it is a fight between groups of the same populations defending their own interests, but who behave as if it was a question of different incompatible biological types, each one looking to seize supremacy and to be in total control, or to exclusively hunt and exterminate the group that hinders their plans. The fact is that Africans have not been able to eliminate the negative view of their quantitative or morphologic variations. But by employing transcendent methodology those variations could avoid becoming a problem that generates more violence, since diversity is one of the basic characteristics of all human populations. (Peace Through African's peaceful Means by Raïs Neza Boneza, kolofon 2004)

As long the promotion of a cultural revenge in the society as the only alternatives in the Rwanda-Burundi-Uganda-Democratic Republic of the Congo conflict will not be removed the cycle of cultural violence is likely to continue endlessly. The consequence will certainly still:

- A seculars, and narrowed presentation of the African dilemma limiting the sources of the conflict to ethnic rivalries, while others factors such social, economical, political, outer-interferences (neo-paternalism) are intertwined in the dynamic of the conflict.
- The philosophy of out-siders and uncontrolled rise of mega-nationalism feeling, that develop a cyclic violence as "who lose the power today, is willing by any means to regain it tomorrow".
- The ideological idea of resolving, internal problems of a state out of his own territory and boundaries. The current tension in the Great Lakes, where Rwanda, Uganda, and Burundi justified the Congo aggression through the allegation that they have to protect their territory against negative forces located in Congo. An establishment of inclusive space of dialogue is prerequisite to the stability of each state.
- The reconstruction of view that perpetuates international prejudice regarding African 'savagery,' that allows the West to escape the responsibility for the severe *structural* damage imposed by colonialism: (1) irrational boundaries that contribute to endemic instability; (2) export-orientated infrastructure that marginalizes Africa within the world economic system; (3) western cultural hegemony that has weakened African tradition; and (4) bureaucratic systems of governance that concentrated political power and favoured certain ethnic groups over others [Griggs 1995].

4. Therapy

Any solution must be transparent, and implicate affected populations. The Secret negotiation among elite actors is unlikely to eliminate the structural factors or latent causes of conflicts. The negotiations must recognise all concerned actors at all level, ethnical group, armed group, civil servants, businessmen and other members of civil society. The fact that Germans under Hitler perpetrated a horrible genocide against in Jews1945 does not imply that every Germans must be executed.

As the violence as destroyed potentiality of trust and truth among people at all level, it is therefore relevant to implement a mechanism of **reconstruction**. The reconstruction dynamic will lead to recall of the potential of culture of peace, which can be use for the **reconciliation process**. The reconciliation process can be even more effective through using endogenous or cultural conflict **resolution** practices such: Gacaca (Rwanda), Ubuntu (South Africa), Kogtla (Kalaharian). E.g. The u*bashingantahe system in traditional Burundi,* which mixed groups of mature, respected Hutus and Tutsis adjudicated disputes a local levels to address certain problems of land reform and reduce the conflict producing discursive practices.

Another alternatives will be to develop a mechanism of regional integration. The region is a receptacle of rebel funds and arms that affect the stability of the region. This fragile network of alliances demands inclusive negotiations based on the needs of the entire region. Political Instability within Congo, The return or a fair integration of refugees, redefinition of nation, states, and reform of laws on nationality must be considered regionally.

Regional organization such the CPGL (the commission for the Great-Lakes Region) could implement structures with a locally based ideal such as the Baraza (Kiswahili word of "Assembly") or the Nyerere's Tanzanian ideal "Ujaama" (Kiswahili word of "Familyhood") that are more easily assimilated by local population.

These local structure well assimilated in the region, could work as dynamic of dismantling the corrupt and inefficient system of hegemonic, and dictatorships powers in the region while expanding participation at a grassroots level. The multiplicity of cultures, ethnic groups and nations makes it a challenge for direct actors but also external-regional actors can help by canalising resources and attention to the plight of Great-lakes region of Africa and promoting inter-cultural understanding. Otherwise history has shown that attempts to democratise along majoritarian lines falter because ruling ethnic groups oppress and oppressed ethnic groups seek power by extra-judicial means.

A bioceanic confederation from the Indian to the Atlantic oceans, including Uganda and Tanzania, Rwanda and Burundi, and the two Congos, maybe more countries, trading East-West with Asia and America, as much as North-South could one of the possible approach as proposed by the

Transcend Network (see www.transcend.org) could allow for decentralisation, softer boundaries, and 'automatic' land reform as people and goods would be free to move. *Not confining people with a tradition of enmity to a very limited territory* and could be accomplished without polemical issues such the redrawing of states borders

As| the boundaries designed by Europeans at the 1884 Berlin Conference have been perpetuated by African leaders since independence. There are no nations in Africa because nearly every state has deep intrastate ethnic divisions. Instead of a fair integration of different ethnical or tribal community, the strongest ethnic group attempts to dominate or to eliminate the others.

One visible consequence of hybridisation which is often neglected in the international and intellectual milieu is the development of a belief in a series of invisible and spiritual forces to elucidate political conflict in Africa. Instead of having direct religious confrontations, Africans have created a mixture of African and western metaphysics (a mix of African, Christian and Islamic religions) which encourages prophetical and spiritual leaders to take an active role in conflicts, since political leaders have failed to establish order.

When talking about metaphysics, we understand a philosophical approach more concerned with the essence of existence, space and time, causes and effects. Through it, people seek to explain events that they see as not rationally explainable. This is because their conception of reality is influenced by their primary hopes, beliefs, feelings, emotions and history added to exogenous elements which differ from their cultural background. These interferences between rationality and normality of the world have given rise to prophetical movements such Mulele, Mai-Mai and Simba's rebellion in ex-Zaire (Kivu); the Holy Spirit Movement of Alice Lakwena and the Lord Resistance Army in Gulu, Uganda (Kony's LRA); the FDD in Burundi, and others. All these movements are characterized by their religious and ritualistic motivation for violence: for example, the baptism of the combatants and a typology of rituals against gun bullets. All of them have spiritual intercessors, or prophetic leaders to interpret signs and the will of

38

the spirits.

Gandhi saw violence as an evil and rational persuasion, and often unavailing, in all cases creating needs and deficits. In Africa, violence expresses itself in various forms. For example, in a physical or psychic way through brainwashing, various forms of indoctrination, threats and intimidations, the only objective is to diminish the spiritual and moral capacities of humans. The violence is directed against the psyche.

Today in Africa, violence is integrated in the political and cultural system; it shapes the skeleton of structural violence as it is manifested in the inequality of relations and opportunities. Also, it is especially expressed as direct violence with actors and agents from both local and international spheres. African civilization is impregnated with a history of violence and degradation. The main ideology in the different conflicts can be summarized with the introduction of the formula "diviser pour mieux regner" or the "divide and conquer" ideology that we shall explore at the macro-cultural level in part III.

CHAPTER III

STRUCTURAL VIOLENCE IN AFRICA

The last decades in Africa have been marred by unprecedented levels of political, ethnic, and transnational conflict. This continent is one of the major battlegrounds of global forces; it is the most marginalized areas of the world. More than thirty wars have been fought in Africa since 1970, and most of these have been internal rather than inter-state wars. In 1996 alone, 14 of the 53 countries of Africa were involved in armed conflicts, and they resulted in more than 8 million refugees and displaced persons. This was before the recent conflict (1996) in the Democratic Republic of Congo which qualifies as an African world war because of the number of countries involved and the four million lives it claimed. The dominant discourse on the causes of conflict in Africa puts emphasis on lack of economic growth and poor governance. It accordingly advocates: (1) the opening up of Africa's economy to foreign capital as a means of improving growth and thus eliminating poverty as a cause of conflict and (2) a more democratic system of governance as a means of encouraging a more inclusive kind of politics.

The real causes of Africa's lack of peace lie precisely in the manner in which Africa has been integrated into the global economy. Through the terms of its integration, Africa has been conditioned to never-ending impoverishment. Only a self-revitalized positive development by the people at the grassroots level and a reshaping of Africa's place in the global economic system can lead to both material growth and peace in Africa.

Two major aspects have played principal roles in the degradation of Africa:

o Micro-cultural aspects: local culture with its diversities, local beliefs, local customs
o Macro-cultural aspects: Globalisation, colonialism, neo-

colonialism, imperialism, imported beliefs (New religions, technology, and economy).

In these two aspects, we shall try to id to ientify the different manifestations of cultural violence. By cultural violence, we mean aspects of culture which can be used to justify or even legitimise direct or structural violence (Peace by Peaceful means 1996, page 196). Despite significant gains in human development from 1960 to 1980, Africa's recent development has been characterized by social, economical, and political crises. Understanding the micro and macro-cultural aspects in the degradation process of Africa will help us to shape out the African archaeology of violence.

When examining the archaeological roots of violence in the African culture in general, we shall identify those aspects in the culture, the symbolic sphere of our existence, exemplified by religion, ideologies, languages and art, empirical and formal science (logical or mathematical) that can be used to justify or legitimise direct or structural violence. Our objective in this presentation is "to follow, look for the root of the thing, matter, and problem" and "to arrange a problem, a matter" as meant by "kuvumbua shida, na ku-badirisha" (Swahili language of eastern Africa), a translation on the Latin dictum: "Bene diagnoscitur, bene curatur. -- "Something that is well diagnosed can be cured well"

In the human sciences, archaeology is the scientific study of past human culture and behaviour, from the origins of humans to the present. Archaeology explores past human behaviour through the examination of material remains of previous human societies; in a similar way, archaeology of violence should be seen as a way to trace traditional cultural elements favouring violence in Africa, using some real examples as samples for our research.

Violence must be identified and evaluated and must confront the tribunal of rationality described by the Kantian formula.

41

* **Conceptual analysis of violence**: violence, observed in all its horrors, must be known and understood, as is emphasized in the TRANSCEND method. An element which destroys then separates what is united. However, to dynamite a field for mineral exploitation is not considered violence. Here, let us regard violence in relation to both human relations and the surrounding environment as destructive.

* **Causality**: the cause of violence here is not a fatality theory, which stipulates that when a country or a region reaches a certain level of demographic development without having at the same time attained a necessary economical development regarding its population, it disintegrates. However, the increasing lack of resources among the peoples is a potential source of violence.

***Typology of violence**: In Peace by Peaceful Means [p.197], Johan Galtung points out the following aspects: survival (killing and exploitation), well-being (maiming, misery, morbidity), identity (alienation, negation), need for freedom (repression, expulsion, marginalization, detention). If the eco-balance for human basic maintenance including survival, well-being, freedom, and identity is not satisfied, we have the tragedy of human degradation.

CHAPTER IV

MICRO-CULTURAL ASPECTS OF VIOLENCE IN AFRICA:

With micro-cultural aspects, we shall concentrate our inquiry on local culture and customs. Africans are divided into several races, fragmented within local communities by ethnic groups, tribal denominations, and clans. These different classifications are expressed in beliefs and customs which shape a ritualistic religion or ideology.

The relationship of religion to both conflict-ridden and pacific social orders from historical, sociological, theological and practical perspectives has contributed to peace and wars as considered in the context of just war, or holy war. In traditional Africa, religious wars did not really develop until the coming of missionaries and the expansion of Islam. We can assert that in the past, religion has been the basis for establishing theocratic states. A theocratic state is a structure. Archaeology is the scientific study of past human culture and behavior, from the origins of humans to the present. Archaeology studies past human behavior through the examination of material remains of previous human societies. Violence is legitimized precisely because it favors those who belong to the state religion and marginalizes those of other faith communities. We see this in the example of President Idi Amin trying to convert Uganda to Islam. Theocracy in Africa should not be seen only as a result of imported religion, but also in the cultural concept of chieftaincy. For example, in the Bantu culture the chief is respected, elevated and seen as representing God or even perceived to be God himself. The result of such conception has given rise to a chronic cycle of dictatorial regimes and the appearance of different "isms," such as Mobutism, Afro-centrism, tribalism, Ndugu-ism, Kabilism, Lumunbism, and others.

Violence in Africa is strongly rooted in the ethnic backgrounds of the members of the community. The belief that one ethnic group is better than another is a classical belief which can be observed even today.

In general, an ethnic group can be described as follows:

A community by appellation and ideology.	A community of values	A community of aspiration or conscience for a given group
Logical explanation from myths and tradition	Culture, codes and customs	That which constitutes the essential elements of existence

The rise of ethnic conflicts in Africa precedes colonization; it is integrated in the whole African social organization. Ethnocentrism is perceived in itself as a flagrant manner or a discriminatory practice of social rejection. In Africa, we are often in the presence of endogenous structural divisions that supply structural or latent violence, expressed through different forms such as swear words, threats, and insults.

* African violence development and the Bantu/Nilotic Myth

1. History of the Virunga (Great-Lakes Region)

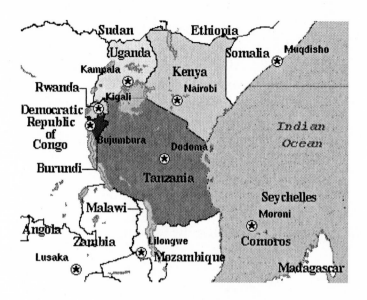

Figure 1 Great lakes of Africa

The first population to inhabit the Virunga region were the Twa, from the Pygmoid peoples of the Congo basin. It is believed that they probably lived in the area for several thousand years. The Twa were hunter-gatherers, dependent on the plant and animal resources of the vast forest for survival. In contrast, the Bantu are physically and culturally different from the Twa. The Bantu were agricultural peoples, using small-scale farming to obtain most of their food. More efficient than the hunting-gathering lifestyle of the Twa, farming allowed the Bantu to live in small communities and to increase quickly in numbers. As the Bantu population increased, more and more of the forests were cleared for crops, an activity that led to the extermination of the Twa.

The Bantu consisted of several tribes, the largest of which is the Hutu in modern-day Rwanda and Burundi; the Shi', Nande, and Buisha in D.R.Congo; and the Baganda, Soga, Nkole, Toro, and Nyoro in modern-day Uganda. Each tribe consisted of several clans, each ruling loosely over a small area. These tribes were numerous and well-established when the next wave of immigrants arrived, this time from the northeast.

The newcomers originated from Ethiopia and Sudan and differed from the established Bantu in many ways. They spoke Nilotic languages; they were taller, thinner. Different from the Bantu, they were pastoral, raising cattle for food. The Nilotics became numerically dominant in the drier savannahs north of Lake Kyoga. These people, often earlier Watutsi, migrated into the Virunga area from the northeast between about 1200 and 1500 A.D. Eventually the Tutsi politically dominated the more numerous Hutu and ruled the area when the Europeans came in force to take over around 1900.

2. The rising of the Nilo/Hamitic ideology

We shall examine the historical origins and political potency of a "mythology" in Africa, especially in the Great Lakes, concerning ethnic or racial distinctions between the Bantu and Nilotic people. The Great Lakes region is composed of Rwanda, Uganda, Burundi, and D.R.Congo; it was, in the pre-colonial period, composed of very highly organized kingdoms such as the Buganda, Bunyoro, Rwanda or Azande. The colonizers did not want to admit that such organization existed in that area. The explorers argued that there must have been an exogenous influence from the Upper Nile.

In the 19th Century, the Hamitic Hypothesis exploded, support by people such as Jhon Speke, an English explorer of the Nile. It was inspired by the biblical tripartite division of the earth's races based on imputed descent from the three sons of Noah – Semites (Arabs and Jews, sons of Shem), Yefites (Europeans, sons of Yafet) and Hamites (black Africans, sons of the cursed Ham) – which had already granted theological imprimatur to the slave trade and apartheid in South Africa. The ideology was supported by German colonialists and Belgian successors after the First World War in Rwanda-Burundi.

The Bantu and Nilotic ideology infects all layers of society in the Great Lakes Region and dominates the thoughts of the average person in the street. It also continues to dominate Western interpretations of the ongoing crisis in the Great Lakes—e.g.the New York Times 1994, deplored a "Rwandan Tribal war between Bantu and Nilotes."

The main lines of the Bantu/hamitic ideology elaborated by the explorers, the missionaries, the theoreticians and agents of the colonial conquest (1):

Burundi and Rwanda are populated by three distinct races: the Bahutu, the Batutsi, and the Batwa. It is important to understand that the term "race" was progressively replaced by "ethnic group" or "tribe", in the media.
- The Bahutu are « farmers (of) Bantu race." These « primitive Bantu » form « the big mass of the population.
- The Batutsi are a « populates ministers hamites, (…) a class of lords conquering, come giants of the north; (they) penetrated the Great Lakes 400 years ago.»
- The Batwa are « the remainders of primitive population of small size and of type pygmoïd, that earn their living as hunters, and as servants to the other population.»

"Beside the physical characteristics of these three « races », there is the « mental characteristic » that distinguish the Mututsi « despotic » Muhutu « servile » and Mutwa «natural wild and overwhelmed due to his social position of outcast »."

Those manipulations of the term Ham for Hamitic, or Kushite, have contributed to building up an African Hitlerist behaviour that has helped enforce the gap between Tutsis and Hutus in Rwanda and Burundi, which ultimately resulted in the 1994 genocide with the minority Tutsis and moderate Hutus as its victims.

3. Afro-Hitlerism

Let us explore the development of cultural violence through some examples from the local languages of the Great Lakes region (Rwanda-Congo-Uganda-Burundi), recalling local words used to justify exclusion and ethnic violence.

3.1. Abatemu in Kinganda (Uganda 1980-1986)

The Ugandan conflict can be explained as a struggle between the southerners and westerners in general, and more specifically as one between the Bantu people and the Northerners (particularly Nilotic Acholi people). Abatemu is a Kiganda word meaning "killers," which has been used to threaten the Acholi ethnic group. Successive governments have promoted that cultural word, which has favoured the installation of a dictatorial regime clothed in a costume of democracy. While fighting in 1980 to topple the Obote government, the current president Museveni recorded in several documents the motivation of his NRM/Army to pursue the war against Obote's UPC This general hostility against the Northerners was quoted in an interview for Drum Magazine in Nairobi during the peace talks of 1984:

"The problem in Uganda is that the leadership has mainly been from the north. The southerners who are mainly Bantu have played a peripheral role all these years since independence in 1962. A lot of blood has been shed. We want genuine elections and we are sure that if these were held the best candidates would win. We are not against the northerners as such and if a popular man from Acholi or Lango or even Madi wins, he will have our mandate. What we cannot stomach is a rigged election, such as the one we had in 1980. We are still prepared to talk to Okello as a military leader on the future of our country but we are not going to talk out of weakness. In fact our forces are already inside Kampala and soon we may surprise the world" (41).

From this statement, we may understand that the fundamental reason for the conflict in Uganda can be explained by a profound misunderstanding between people who have the same land in common. This cultural hostility has initiated a cycle of several civil wars, such us the current one by Kony's LRA (Lord Resistance

Army), a movement whose abducted children have been categorized by the U.S. government as "international terrorists."

3.2. Kulo Kwor ; Acholi (Uganda-Sudan)

In the monographic thesis by Professor Gingyera Pinyewa, the custom of Kulo Kwor is a recipe for a cultural, intra-familiar and community practice of violence which implies retaliation. He explains that Kulo Kwor is retribution, a legitimised use of vengeance among the Acholis. He has attributed the killings and burning of villages to that practice. Literally, Kulo means "to pay" or "to give," especially blood compensation; and Kwar means "life that has been killed." This practice is observed in several pastoral communities throughout the Nile Basin, such as Ethiopians and Somalis.

3.3. Ynyenzi in Kinyarwanda (Rwanda 1964-1994), or "The Theory of the cockroaches"

In Rwanda, Ynyenzi is a word that contributed the separation this country's society at the beginning of independence in the 1960's, when the minority ethnic group lost its formal privileges to the benefit of the majority. Ynyenzi, meaning "cockroaches," was used to designate the rebels, but that created a prejudice against one entire ethnic group, the Tutsi minority.

3.4. Nteramwe in kinyarwanda (1993 Rwanda-Burundi)

Nteramwe at the beginning of 1993 was a word meaning "togetherness," literally "people who make things together." The MRND political party in power in Rwanda that year used the word to create a militia group to unite forces against the rebel invasion from Uganda. Nevertheless, after the Rwandan genocide of 1994, the word has been used to designate one ethnic group, the Hutu majority. This contributed to the imposition of an international cultural and intellectual embargo on one ethnic group seen as the promoter of massacre and genocide. Today it is almost impossible for a Hutu to seek asylum in another country. Considering events and history in the Great-Lakes region of Africa, the Rwandan-Burundi case is comparable to a cultural Hitlerism that has contributed to jeopardize one or both ethnic groups by creating a cycle of hatred. The Great Lakes region reacts as a matrix in East and central Africa because the conflict and culture are inter-twined, which explains the escalation of violence in the Sub-Saharan region of Africa.

3.5. Nduguism in Swahili (East D.R.Congo 1990)

The word Nduguism appeared in the late 1990s in the eastern part of D.R.Congo with the uprising of ethnic clashes between locals and those considered to be Rwando-phone communities in the ex-Zaire. Unfortunately, Nduguism (14) is not a Congolese speciality, but a global sub-Saharan ideology, which implies a different kind of nepotism (clan, tribal), racism, ethno-tribalism, and self-inflicted African apartheid in these societies. That ideology is exemplified in Zimbabwe, where leaders used a racist and Afro-centrist behaviour to brutalize peasants for their own interest.
43.6. "La theorie de la vermine"or"The Theory of the Vermin" (D.R.Congo 1996)

This was promoted by the Kabilist government after toppling the Mobutist regime. It contributed to igniting ethnic hatred in the D.R.Congo, especially in the eastern part of the country. Many people have been forced to leave the country and lose their nationality. In other cases, the ethnic clashes between Lendu and Hema since 1998, in the northeast of Congo (Bunia), which are another version of the Rwandan genocide, have inflicted further damage on the local structure of the populations, and reduced the potential of survival in the region.

The conflict in Sub-Saharan countries is not a simple fight for power, as would be the case between two opposed political parties or a simple fight between tribes or ethnic groups; rather, it is a fight between groups of the same populations defending their own interests, but who behave as if it was a question of different incompatible biological types, each one looking to seize supremacy and to be in total control, or to exclusively hunt and exterminate the group that hinders their plans. The fact is that Africans have not been able to eliminate the negative view of their quantitative or morphologic variations. But by employing transcendent methodology those variations could avoid becoming a problem that generates more violence, since diversity is one of the basic characteristics of all human populations.

People of different ethnic groups can coexist peacefully and at the end coalesce into a new political or social entity. Therefore, it is not only a fight between supposed ethnic entities that describes the African dilemma; we must not forget the ethnic-endogenous and pre-colonial racism that has been reinforced by hexogen agents imported by colonialism and internalized by the autochthonous communities.

* The different theories and their relation to gender

"When you educate a man you educate an individual. When you educate a woman you educate a nation." Malcolm X

Women are unfortunate to have grown up for many generations in societies that considered God as male. A woman never has her identity affirmed as a reflection of the divine if she lives in a society of a Father God. In trying to explore this aspect, I am not trying to give any sexual identity to a given Divinity. But through exploring culture, history and development, we are trying to explain an aspect that cannot be neglected, especially in terms of repairing African societies. In this view, women and men must realize that divinity has a female aspect as well – that for thousands of years ancient cultures worshiped goddesses. As a first step for their empowerment in Africa as well as other parts of world, women might begin to experiment with the sacred side of their femininity in their own life, to see the divine in themselves and themselves in the divine.

According to Robert Graves (English poet and classical scholar, 1895-1985), the earliest societies and religions were matriarchal.

The moon (female) was thought to control the sun (male). In the Bantu culture, today it is said that Women are the stronghold in the education of society.

In contemporary Africa, societies have forgotten and hidden the highest position of the Queen Mother, Mother Earth, and the Goddess. Diodorus of Sicily, who had visited Egypt some time between 60 and 56 BC, writes that the Egyptians had a law "permitting men to marry their sisters" and that "it was ordained that the queen should have greater influence and honor than the king and that among private persons the wife should enjoy authority over her husband."

I am not suggesting that women should rule over men, or vice versa, but a complementary relationship between the male and female principles is a way to harmonize and to perfect our societies. If Africa is the cradle of humanity, then we can extrapolate that African women gave birth to humanity. In ancient Africa, the Queen Mother was the source of the royal right to office because she embodied the people's wisdom. The dowry granted by the husband's family to the bride's family was a guarantee that a woman was valued, treasured, respected, and an essential member of the family, village and nation. In the 5th century B.C., Herodotus, who had visited Egypt, writes that "women buy and sell; the men abide at home and weave."

In The African Origin of civilizations: Myth or Reality (1983) by Dr. Cheik Anta Diop; it is stated that:

Female dominated system of society with descent through the female line is the basis of the social organisation in Egypt and throughout Black Africa. In sharp contrast there has never been any proof of the existence of a paleo-Mediterranean matriarchy supposedly exclusively white. The absence of queens in Greek, Roman or Persian history should be noted and yet in stark contrast during those remote epochs, queens were frequent in Black Africa. Negro matriarchy is as alive today as it was during Antiquity. In regions where the matriarchy system has not been altered by external influences (Islam) it is the woman who transmits political rights – heredity is effective only matrilineal.

Another typical aspect of African matriarchy is the dowry paid by the man, a custom reversed in European counties. The woman holds a privileged position in Africa and so it is she who receives a guarantee in the form of a dowry in the alliance called marriage. Thus if the marriage is broken off it is to the man's disadvantage

A few thousand years ago, many goddess-oriented civilizations were destroyed by aggressive Indo-European tribes who worshipped aggressive sky gods, and females lost their sacredness. That is an essential ingredient in the invasion of Africa by the newer monotheistic world religions: Judaism, Islam, and Christianity, whose one god is male. It also took shape in the Iron Age, when men dominated societies in Europe and the Middle East. The origins of patriarchal systems in Africa, and elsewhere, are a consequence of an infamy or sacrilege resulting from the brutal violation of the sacred. Marduk, the Babylonian patriarchal figure, murders his mother Tiamat and forms the cosmos from her body; similarly, Tlaloc, the patriarchal rain god of the Aztecs, began the foundation of the world by murdering his mother as soon as he was born from her body. In Greek mythology, myths describing the rise of Zeus over the Titans, have many sexual conquests; the rape of Persephone by Hades, the slaying of the Medusa by Perseus, and the slaying of the Sphinx by Oedipus, depict a transition from matriarchy to patriarchy.

In conclusion, peace building is a process that must be participatory. Therefore, men as well as women must be involved in the process. A bird (society) with one wing (gender) can not fly as it is said. Women play an equally important role in the resolution of conflicts. In the "Kogtla" process (Kalahari Desert, Namibia; south Africa. see below), the Bushmen are conscious of this, and women are not excluded. In contrast to certain tribes that don't give the credence to women, the Bushmen promote participation of both genders in handling their community matters. An old African story explains mythically that "the reasons why many wars kill women, children and the elderly is because women give birth to those who will become the future soldiers and when they kill the women, they eliminate the children-to-be that would grow to be soldiers and take revenge. By killing the elders, they erase the memory of the past about how things were."

My brief opinion is that African women are victimized by an African cultural sexism that has been passed down and is still being practiced as part of a normal and acceptable culture in African society. Gender issues are contradictory to the usual cultural discourse that promotes respect and dignity of women, and still not a priority for African societies. African societies must work hard to end repression of women and to promote an appropriate representation at all levels by women.

CHAPTER V

MACRO-CULTURAL ASPECTS

Four forces have been major cause of the development of violence in the African macro-cultural level: religion, technology, economy, and empires. These have not always acted separately and often have supported each other. For example, the expansion of Christianity started with the conversion of Emperor Constantine I of Rome in the year 313. The religious conversion of an emperor started the process under which Christianity became the dominant religion not only in Europe but also in several other societies later ruled or settled by Europeans, including Africa. The expansion of Islam began not with converting a ready-made empire, but with building an empire almost from scratch. The Umayyad and Abbasids dynasties put together bits of other people's empires (e.g., former Byzantine Egypt and former Zoroastrian Persia) and created a completely new civilization. Prof. E. Possoz of Brussels, Bantu Philosophy, made the following important observation: up to the present, ethnographers have denied all abstract thought to tribal people (Africans). The civilised Christian ("colonist") people were exalted, while the savage and primitive man ("African") was denigrated and defamed. The theory of colonisation is based on this concept.

V.1. Theory of colonization: "diviser pour mieux regner" in Africa

The Berlin Conference was Africa's undoing in more ways than one. The colonial powers superimposed their domains on the African continent. By the time independence returned to Africa in 1950, the realm had acquired a legacy of political fragmentation that could neither be eliminated nor made to operate satisfactorily. (de Blij, p.340).

In 1884, at the time of the conference, only the coastal areas of Africa were colonized by the European powers. At the Berlin

55

Conference the European colonial powers scrambled to gain control over the interior of the continent. This new map of the continent was imposed and disregarded the cultural and linguistic boundaries already established by the indigenous African population.

By 1914, the conference participants had fully divided Africa among themselves into fifty countries:

* Great Britain desired a Cape-to-Cairo collection of colonies and almost succeeded though their control of Egypt, Sudan (Anglo-Egyptian Sudan), Uganda, Kenya (British East Africa), South Africa, and Zambia, Zimbabwe, and Botswana (Rhodesia). The British also controlled Nigeria and Ghana (Gold Coast).
* France took much of western Africa, from Mauritania to Chad (French West Africa) and Gabon and the Republic of Congo (French Equatorial Africa).
* Belgium and King Leopold II controlled the Democratic Republic of Congo (Belgian Congo).
* Portugal took Mozambique in the east and Angola in the west.
* Italy's holdings were Somalia (Italian Somaliland) and a portion of Ethiopia.
* Germany took Namibia (German Southwest Africa) and Tanzania (German East Africa).
* Spain claimed the smallest territory - Equatorial Guinea.

The authoritarian character of governance in African countries perpetuated by Belgian, French, British and Portuguese colonial rule was not overcome by the post-independence regimes. Militarism reinforced authoritarian rule and favoured an economic injustice which resulted from the failure of governments to redress economic imbalances between the members of local communities. For example, between Tutsi and Hutu (Rwanda-Burundi), Northerners and Westerners (Uganda), Baganla and Baswahili (R.D.Congo, Ex-Zaire), Arab and Black in Sudan, and generally throughout Nilotic and Bantu in Africa.

The development of a free market economy also favoured foreign and local exploiters of the poor. The free market adoption imported new alien behaviours and words to the African culture, such as corruption and prostitution, which reinforced a social and cultural oppression that is characterised by nepotism, ethnic chauvinism, sectarianism and discrimination.

Ethnic problems that are constant in the African corporations are an artificial phenomenon maintained by those who need to satisfy their political and economic appetites. All ethnic, tribal or clan differentiations in Africa are very volatile because Africans usually identify themselves with a particular group, based on family tradition and reputation. One is Ashanti or Zulu because we have learned it from our family, mother, father, and brothers or because the neighbouring environment identifies it.

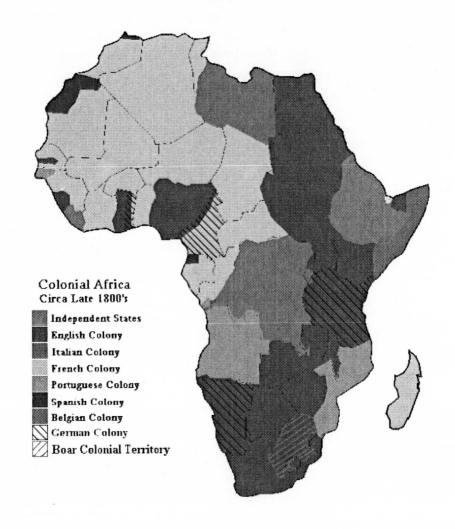

Figure V. 1.1Colonial Africa, Source:

http://www.globalissues.org/Geopolitics/Africa/Intro.asp

V.2. what can we do about it?

It is necessary to save the fragments that remain of the population structures. It is also necessary to make sure that violence does not become an epidemic for Africa. African intellectuals and their colleagues in other continents must analyze the problem in all its dimensions, beyond simple opportunistic manipulations. The African problem clearly must be questioned by disciplines that are uninfluenced by military-economic pressures. The development of a theoretical basis may be the beginning of a durable political and educational solution.

Meanwhile some positive initiatives have been taken by African states to resolve the crisis that maintains them behind the global transformations process. For example, the N.E.P.A.D (The New Partnership for Africa's Development) is a vision and strategic framework for Africa's renewal; its objectives are to eradicate poverty; to bring African states onto a path of sustainable growth and development; to halt the marginalisation of Africa in the globalisation process and enhance its full and beneficial integration into the global economy; and to accelerate the empowerment of women.

It may be necessary to work on of a process of international cooperation to help African states reach their goal through the N.E.P.A.D. We know that conflict appears when there is an unbalance in the needs among the members of a given society. The present area of study consists of investigating the different problems in social and cultural settlement Africa that will allow citizens to understand and work more effectively in strengthening a foundation of a lasting peace in the continent.

Africa can be seen as some kind of ambassador of the poor in the world. The daily deep poverty in which African families struggle, can only generate more conflicts. Insecurity and instability are common problems for most states in Africa; as well as uansett - the diverse cultural backgrounds of African people.

Ordinary individual are victimized by increase violence and a moral global economy that only benefits a Groupuscule elite class of the rich. The propagation of violence in the continent has destroyed most of the former structures inherited from colonisation and earlier times. The result is the killing and impoverishment of innocent people..

The large majority of the states are lead by dictatorial rulers that clothe themselves in the trappings of democracy. The power is either military or monolithic: one group tries to preserve power using violence, corruption, and other cynical abuses and crimes. Poverty and brutality are the daily reality for the population. In the African reality, great advantage is taken of widespread illiteracy and ignorance. In this society of despotic, fanatic and corrupt rulers, many people perish from the lack of knowledge.

War always starts in the minds of people when there is a sudden appearance of lack of trust in the society. When people consider each other as potential enemies, then racism, xenophobia and other types of clan nepotism follow.

Poverty and Underdevelopment Factors:

Historical Factors
Cultural and social factors
Economic factors
Political factors
Late internal rivalities

Poor-cultural investment
Poor infrastructure or urbanisation development
Poor institutional development
Slavery
High illiteracy and Ignorance
Global economy and capital market
Inequitable economical distribution
Colonization Diviser pour mieux regner

High Population Growth
Aid dependence-external debt problem
Political immaturity and weak leadership

A vitalizing Transcendental Culture as proposed by Galtung [p.208 In Peace By Peaceful Means], through the establishment of a new academic field which he calls Culturology: the science of human culture, would enable us to move towards a culture of peace. Transcendental Culturology will allow us to extract the different areas of our culture and our mentality that contain a potential for violence to create possible peaceful interaction between cultures and civilizations. De betyr; we must identify the structural violence in local corporations and cultures and be conscious of the racist and fascist ideologies introduced into our Bantu-Nilo-Hamitic vision.

The African dilemma has given rise to five types of cultural feelings:

-       Shame to be African.
-       Shame to be Black,
-       Self-slavery,
-       Humiliation
-       Victimization.

These feelings tend to be a kind of nihilism which implies that humans are born as perverted animals instead of the rational beings defined by the Greek philosophers. This nihilism has created a failure of human reason and civilization for the benefit of barbarism.

CHAPTER VI

TRANSCENDING CULTUROLOGY AS A SCIENCE OF CULTURAL PEACE

It is essential to analyze civilizations (rather than states), or economic or political systems, as units, in the spirit of seeking solutions rather than making condemnations. Even if the deep roots of violence and war are part of the cosmology which in turn is collective and subconscious, there may be ways of breaking the collective into sub-collectives and individuals and ways of making the subconscious conscious.

As cultural peace is the aspect in a culture that justifies or directs peace or structural peace, violence is the animalistic manner of resolving conflicts, while dialogue and negotiation are the only human manners to resolve conflict. Transcendental culturology opens a new field of dialogue using existing archaeological, linguistic, and socio-anthropological science as the departure point for dialogue and negotiation between civilizations. It is necessary to believe and to work on the possibility that humanity will be able one day, after a process of self-education, to overcome the social character of violence as a destructive collective behaviour.

Indeed we are not Zulu, Bemba, Woloff, and Amarick by nature or by the blood that circulates in our veins, but by our inherited cultural package and history. Therefore, the current barbarism in Africa and in the rest of the world can only be explained historically, and culturally but not naturally, or racially as the pessimistic conceptual tendency of humanity tends to explain it.

Guided by an optimistic conception, our contribution in Swahili is the words ku-badirisha, "to arrange the matter." We recommend dialogue and negotiation in each state that has been affected by conflict crises. The establishment of "Truth and Reconciliation" forum following the example of South Africa would facilitate public dialogue. To re-shape Africa will require that protagonists and antagonists accept and examine the cultural history of their countries, to build and strengthen the African societies without the influence of any "Politique d'Autruche."

* Example of cultural Peace in The Sub-Saharan region of Africa

1. Kahalarian or Khoisan wisdom: « kgotla »

When a serious problem arises in the community, men and women meet to sit and talk. Everyone is invited to participate without any segregation. The « kgotla », as it is called by the khoisan people (**San** for the Bushmen or **Hottentots**)and, is a completely open discussion and that can last until the quarrel is resolved. During the talk, no member of the group is authorized to leave if the problem is not yet resolved. They go so far as to bring back a person who has left before they have found a solution.

Reaction of the community facing the threat of violence.

Khoisan people manage the protagonists, who can easily kill each other since everyone possesses poisoned arrows, by:

- Disarmament: The first group confiscates the poisoned arrows and hides them somewhere in bush,
- Mediation: The second group separates the belligerents.
- Dialogue: The groups come together, and discussion and sharing start. The objective of the « kgotla » consists of finding a viable solution that will be acceptable by the protagonists and by the community.
- Reconciliation and reconstruction: After being assured that the misunderstanding does not exist anymore between protagonists, the elder officially announces the end of the conflict.

In cases of conflict involving a person that does not belong to the groups, the "San" proceed almost in same manner, by asking the person concerned to attend. If he or she does not come, the group delegates people to move and bring the person to them.

2. Baraza

Baraza is a Swahili word meaning "gathering", or "table of dialogue." Baraza in the traditional society was used to settle differences and conflicts. It symbolized a traditional assembly led by a council of elders and wise ones. People in conflict were brought there to arrange and resolve their problems. In the eastern region of Africa, former antagonists were asked to bring with them gifts for each other. Accepting to go to baraza meant that we were going to solve the problem and restore the harmony in the relation between our clan, family and community. Baraza was employed in the case of apartheid under the name of the Commission of Truth and Reconciliation.

3. Gacaca in Kinyarwanda (Rwanda 1997-2001)

The Gacaca was a participatory restorative tribunal of justice parallel to the International Criminal Tribunal for Rwanda established by the U.N Council in November 1994. The Gacaca jurisdiction in general was adopted to fight impunity by introducing community service and promoting reconciliation. With Gacaca, the Rwandan community had the following objectives:

* To encourage confessions,
* To solve the problem of overcrowding in prisons and reduce the pressure on the state budget,
* To participate in the social rehabilitation of the inmates and use this workforce to contribute to the development of the country.

Gacaca was a real example of communal justice as opposed to mob justice and retaliation. By avoiding the usual punitive justice, it promotes restoration and reconstruction. Unfortunately, Gacaca fails in some ways because of political influence and because participant in the genocide residing in Rwanda did not attend the cultural court. The failure could have also resulted from the lack of support or involvement of the international community probably due to several political factors.

64

3. Kacoke Madit, Acholi ethnic groups (Sudan- Uganda)

This is a sort of "table ronde" of dialogue and a form of reconciliation in Acholi culture that unites elders, peasants, intellectuals and religious leaders, including a coalition of chiefs. In the example of the "West African talk under the Baobab", an arena of sharing and talk between generations and classes, Kacoke Madit literally means"umbrella." Like the Baobab tree, the umbrella symbolises here a refreshing shelter from the burden and hardships of the climate, hot sun, rain etc. represented by conflict and social turbulence.

Cultural peace implies that the violence occurring in Africa, and in the world in general, is opposed to rationalism. To be rational in regard to peace and social behaviour is to advocate the supremacy of dialogue, negotiation, and non-violence. In his comment in 1980, L.S.Senghor, then President of Senegal, (2) said," the international Progress Organization chose to treat... a problem that appears for me to be the major complexity of the latter quarter of the 20TH century." The new world-wide economical order must attain two objectives, that, for us, are dramatically linked : to transform the world and change life so that the human, better nourished, better clothed, better educated, stronger and beautiful, may be more human and to accomplish this new humanism, the participation of everyone is needed because the task is rough, but challenging." (Preface by Léopold Sédar Senghor, President of the Republic of Senegal, to I'S. P. O." book one the International New Economic Order, 17 July 1980).

CHAPTER VII

THE DARK OR FORGOTTEN CONTINENT?

"Africa is a nation that suffers from incredible disease, and it suffers from poverty, as well."
(President George W. Bush speaking at the European Union summit in Gothenburg, Sweden on June 14, 2001). Through these words of President Bush, we can remark that Africa is not recognized as a vast and diverse continent; three times bigger than the United States, it is commonly treated as a single entity. In addition to longstanding stereotypes that depict Africa as primitive and dangerous, such forces as limited or biased media coverage and uninformed statements by public officials reinforce the impression in Africa and the world that the entire African continent is impoverished, disease-ridden, and rife with brutal and intractable conflict. In 1965, Galtung & Ruge established a model of selective gate-keeping designed to deal with factors that determined the selection and alteration of certain events. These are:

- Intensity: where matters of 'national interest' have more priority than matters of a regular level of significance,
- Cultural proximity: the closer the event to the culture and interests of the target audience, the more likely its selection.
- Continuity: once an event has been declared 'newsworthy,' it is more likely to be supported in the media, pushing other issues off the agenda.

Figure on Coverage of wars and conflicts in Africa by International
TV News programs 2000-2003:

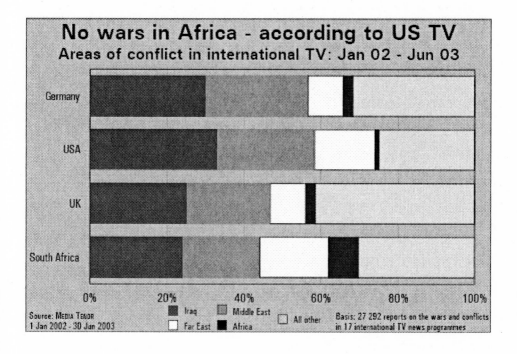

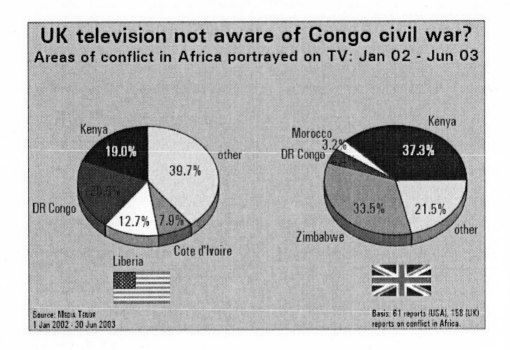

UK television not aware of Congo civil war?
Areas of conflict in Africa portrayed on TV: Jan 02 - Jun 03

Kenya 19.0%
other 39.7%
DR Congo
12.7% 7.9%
Cote d'Ivoire
Liberia

Morocco 3.2%
DR Congo
Kenya 37.3%
33.5% 21.5%
other
Zimbabwe

Source: MEDIA TENOR
1 Jan 2002 - 30 Jun 2003

Basis: 61 reports (USA), 158 (UK) reports on conflict in Africa.

SOURCE: ABC, CBS, NBC; BBC, ITV; ARD, ZDF, RTL. 2002 - 2003, 27 292 reports on conflicts, New African, 377:16-27;
Galtung, J. & Ruge, M.H. 1965. The structure of foreign news.

CHAPTER VIII

THE PATH TO A CULTURAL DEMOCRACY IN AFRICA

If we study African cultures, we learn that there is no proper translation of the word "democracy" nor of the word "dictator." Africa has not been set apart from the world's evolution. The origin of the word democracy is in the Greek words demos, "the people," and cratos "the power or the government." In this sense, there is no match for that word in other European languages either. Both the African term Demokrasia (in Swahili), and the word "democracy" in English are borrowed from Greek.

To better understand the hardships that we encounter when trying to experience an intercultural approach, we must try to study the process of the birth and development or relationship between two given cultures in contact in space and time. For example, Scandinavia with its geographic and climatic space, its own customs, history, social or political structures, is very different from the Great Lakes region in Africa. Therefore, the European languages such as Norwegian, Swedish, English, French and others, have inherited a common Northen birthplace in a temperate or Nordic climate, much of whose literature, art and expressions are related and held in common. The Greek language sharing the same geo-space, made from the same geo-elements (such as winter, snow, cypresses etc.) do not really have equivalents in Swahili, Bambara, Kinyarwanda or other African languages of the Sub-Saharan region. Many Europeans will not encounter strong difficulties communicating with each other on a basic relationship, artistic or literary expression or political or scientific level.

Tilte or words such The "Little White Snow" (Sneewittchen, 1857 Gebrüder Grimm), or "A rose by any other name would smell as sweet" by W.Shakespeare. It would be very difficult to translate the same words into African languages. It might then possible to use expressions or images that are universal and detached from geo-space and cultural-spaces. For example, The Dukke Hjem,

1879 (A Doll's House) by the famous Norwegian writer Henrik Ibsen has been translated into almost all European languages and that could fit in African languages as oppression of women is common in Africa.

What about demos-cratos?

The analysis of some figures could present the African people from being cast into a stream of darkness while the world (especially the western world) seems to be engaged in a crusade against civilizations considered to be backwards and barbaric.

Many Africans consider the Western model of political democracy to be extremely narrow and even alien to African cultures. There are some African thinkers who called upon an invention of an African-style democracy rooted in cultural and original customs of the so-called Dark Continent. But democracy is not about just voting and seizing power but the duty of every citizen to accept responsibility for her/his own society. The European imposition of democracy on the people of Africa without regard to the cultural background and customs seems to favour unnecessary competition and antagonism. In an African geo-space and cultural-space vision, democracy seems to signify, a spreading of diverted ideas although Africans today are in need of converted ideas.

To democratise Africa needs not only the creation of many parties, but also a forum for the exchange of ideas by strengthening the civil society, stability, and peace; a society infused with a spirit of liberty, justice, and equality. Although the words democracy and dictator do not really exist in our languages, words for liberty, justice, equality do exist. Those are the foundations of a democratic society.

Therefore, Africans need to define for themselves the meaning of democracy in their own historical and cultural contexts, drawing on their participatory traditions and the experience of democratic societies elsewhere. Capitalism, globalisation, free-market, and multi-partism are not synonymous of democracy; the respect of human dignity, social, civil or economical rights is a basic premise if democracy must take place in Africa. Democracy cannot exist in Africa or anywhere when the gap between poor and rich is deep and profound.

Overview of Africa

Does democracy exist in Africa? And what does it look like? Let us try to explore the political development in that continent from the end of the Cold War from 1989 to 1990. Strangled by authoritarian regimes, most of them supported by western powers, Africa saw several movements and massive demonstrations calling for a new political order of more freedom or liberty. As a consequence of these pressures, more than 60 leaders lost their position during the period up to 1995. In that political abyss, the Organization of African Unity (OAU) showed its weakness, as a majority of state members in that organization are still in conflict.

The quest for democracy in Africa means a search for human dignity expressed in Swahili as heshima, liberty as Uhuru, Unity as Umoja, right as haki. It is a quest for the liberation of men and women from every kind of servitude as Utumwa, discriminations as Ubaguzi, injustice as Udhalimu, and humiliations as haibu in Swahili. It is an undisputable fact that democracy, along with a handful of other concerns such as health (Afia), development (maendeleo) and peace (Amani), has become one of the core and foremost pre-occupations of the people of the world today; everywhere people are demanding their rights.

Then what is the meaning of democracy?

In a small city far from the African coast, Athens (Greece); demo-kratos; Demos means people and Kraten or Kratos means govern. An equivalent in Swahili (African language) would be Kratos for Utawala and Demos for Watu. The definition of President Abraham Lincoln, USA, of democracy was of a government of the people; by the people; for the people.

71

For the African definition of the term was expressed by President Olessegun Obassanjo of Nigeria while participating in 1989 in the conference of Democratic Revolution in Washington, D.C. He said:

"Periodic elections of political leadership through the secret ballot; popular participation of all adults in the election process; choice of programmes and personalities in the elections; an orderly succession, openness of the society; an independent judiciary; freedom of ownership; institutional pluralism; a democratic culture and democratic spirit and fundamental human rights."

What about democracy in African Society before Colonialism?

Many African scholars have argued that traditional African society was harmonious and based on a certain practice of free expression among the elders. Although domestic slavery existed, African family life was based on unity, freedom, responsibility and equality.

The African conception of freedom cannot be separated from responsibility. Property ownership was governed by the same egalitarian principles and there could be no individually hoarded wealth while others starved in poverty. There were no exploiting classes. African traditional life was a socialist one, as late President Nyere argued, and that inequality only set in with the advent of the capitalist money economy during colonialism, when this delightful harmony of egalitarianism was disrupted.

In my view, it is elusive to try to describe those traditional systems as democratic, because we do not have that word in our mother tongues, or the word dictator. The root must be found in the African philosophy and conception of power, grandeur, and honour. In effect, many pre-colonial African regimes were certainly authoritarian, such as those of the emperors of Rwabugiri in Rwanda, the Kabakas of Uganda, Shaka the Zulu Chief or Nsiri in Congo. But for example, a country such as Botswana incorporating the traditional system of elders into a modern constitution is a clear testimony of original African democracy.

Conclusion:

Africa today is in a situation where superpowers compete for zones of influence. Africa today does not need to define democracy or to construct an African type of democracy, since the basics of democracy (words such dignity, peace, unity, harmony, justice or tolerance) have existed in our languages for several decades. Africans need stability, the time to grow food, to progress and develop. The road to democracy is gradual, and the tenet in the democracy process is to promote peace, development, and encourage political pluralism and tolerance. Since we have difficulties defining it in an African way, then let us focus on the foundation of democracy which has a universal image: freedom, respect for human rights, peace and development. Citizens should be aware that to expect a perfect democracy is not realistic. Based on their experiences and reflections on the basic tenets of life, Africans must consider the application of democracy as a challenge and an opportunity to create healthy relationships in society, as agents of change with the ultimate goal of continually improving democracy and building peace.

And for Africa the task can be described as follows:

On the Micro Level:

Free exposition of the problem
Free expression and discussion in society
Dialogue and reconciliation
Equality of gender
Emphasis on the use of non-violent means
Support of peace initiatives through education and culture
Always a creative search for a solution that will be satisfying for both sides in their disagreement
Support of regional cooperation as a means for the non-discriminatory liberalization of multilateral trade and stability in

societies
Regional integration initiatives and sustainability
Democracy; good political, economic and corporate governance

This means the need to develop arenas such as "Truth and Reconciliation, Baraza, Gashasha, ku-Badirisha."

*on the macro level

Equal opportunity regarding international treaties
Support for local African development initiatives such as the NEPAD
Support of a direct integration of Africa in the global process
A revision of the African debt to alleviate poverty
Help in investing more resources in healthcare, education and culture for development
Reduction and control of the supply of arms and ammunitions sold and used in Africa
Neo-independence

In conclusion, African governments and international economic or social activists must concentrate more resources on education and art to reduce ignorance, misery, and the spread of violence. That will enhance the humanistic thought of the late poet and President Leopold de Sedar Senghor of Senegal; "Le Rendez-vous du donnez et du recevoir" meaning "the meeting of giving and receiving." We firmly believe that education is the only key to liberate Africa from the ingrained mentalities of auto-destruction, self-abuse and self-hatred. It is the only way to eradicate the collective ignorance, the inferiority complex, the colonial mentality and mental slavery. Africa is in dire need of that missing link, and that missing link is "education", and we mean the kind of education that is far beyond bogus titles.

CHAPTER XI

Final Conclusion: "Amani na Salama" as Final draft of an African culture of peace

In conclusion, this work calls for peace through African traditionnal peaceful means for the continent. Amani (Swahili; Central and East-Africa) means an absence of turbulence, all threatening action from internal or external origin, but the word which expresses the essence finality of the amani definition of peace is salama: quietness, concord and harmony. These two words symbolise Maisha, meaning life itself. Amani and Salama are opposite to vita (conflict, war, violence) and vita is opposite to Maisha (life).

In Africa, for both humans and animals, there exists a notion of basic self-preservation of the individual. For example, we need food and forcibly so we kill the cow to have meat, we dynamite the field to extract minerals, or we pull out fruits and plants to have Food; those are, with certain limits, necessary and inevitable. This is what I call a bio-phile type of violence symbolized in the Bushi as (U-muziro), different from the necrophile type of violence that destroys life (U-mugoshe). Humans are the only animals that can kill their own species with no rational profit, or biological necessity or economical profit.

Africa has the ingredients for both cultural peace and violence. In identifying both these two characteristics, we can conclude that it is possible to create an environment of Amani, Salama, and Maisha embedded in the African concept of Ubuntu. Ubuntu ideas promote and sustain human and institutional capacity-building in the field of culture and socio-economic development. It is intended to strengthen cross-cultural understanding and international co-operation as the humanistic message of the late President of Senegal L.S.Senghor stated: "Le rendez-vous du donnee et du recevoir", the meeting of giving and receiving between civilizations.

SUPPLEMENTS

NOTICE

The three following essays and presentations in this part are intended to give a backgrounds of the ideas from which Peace by African's peaceful means is rooted. The focus here will be to learn about African cultures in general.

As the reader may have observed, the present work is inspired *by* Peace *by Peaceful Means, 1996*, by Prof. Johan Galtung, the father of peace studies and leader of the TRANSCEND Network, a global movement dedicated to peace building and the non-violent means of conflict resolution.

My view is that Peace research has made great advances in the Twentieth Century. We are able to define positive peace as well as negative peace. In other words, we now have a more global perspective on the causes of violence. The concerns are now beyond peace-making (conflict resolution and conflict management) and include peacekeeping, and peace building. Africa is in urgent need of the TRANSCEND method, which has a universalistic view without any geo-space limitations. Therefore this work could be the first draft in edifying the Transcend Method in building peace in Africa through reviving mature civil in grass roots society.

SUPPLEMENT 1

WORLD CITIZEN'S DEMOCRACY

BY RAIS NEZA BONEZA

The new millennium is still profoundly affected by the bloodshed and conflicts of the 20th century. The world seems to be in a continual state of rebellion. The condition of people in our age, 15 years after the end of the Cold War, is still unhappiness, the incapacity to decide for ourselves, general despair, and uncertainty in daily life, all embodied in the lack of one principle, "Democracy."

How can we apply democracy to millions or billions of people?

Many of the leaders in totalitarian systems or former colonised countries like those of Africa have responded to this question. The late General Mobutu Sese Seko from the Democratic Republic of Congo legitimised his dictatorships by recalling the return to African authenticity. Leaders in China choose not to understand how more than a billion of people in their country could be given the right to express themselves freely. For those leaders, freedom and democracy rhyme with chaos.

Nowadays we call ourselves civilised, but all humanity is in complete turbulence. International relations are mined by a spirit of competition that creates a climate of anxiety and hostility. The system controlled by a minority of the world population is growing more and more greedy and powerful. This can suppress all hope of realizing ideals in the citizens who are "overwhelmed" and frustrated by the decision-making group. Society has lost the centre of its values. People are living under the threat and fantasy of extinction, terrorism, chemical weapons, and nuclear danger, the indicators of unresolved domestic conflicts.

For the sake of particular perversions of democracy, we sacrifice people and ignore the meaning of democracy which lies in freedom and the respect of human dignity; the foundation of which world identified in the almost cultural-religious dogma: "love your neighbour."

The disease of stereotypes gnaws all civilisations around the world, creating conflict classes, different groups and denominations. The individual is swallowed up in the herd; humans are dehumanised, losing their selfhood.

The September 11 attack on the United States completely transformed the face of the world. There is no negotiation, no dialogue; only the rationale of the strongest. The fear among us is stronger, and perhaps stronger than it ever has been. International laws still form a mere border between hostility and stability.

How can we stabilise and develop our world?

Democracy is the key, but how can we apply democracy centuries after Athens, to not only one small community or city but to billions of people with different cultural backgrounds and achnowledging the equality of gender? How to understand freedom and human dignity? Could peace be possible after all?

Justice is the answer

The new meaning of democracy – Humans try to resolve the difficulties of existence when confronted by nature and human inter-relationships. Human creates morality, religion, art, politics or economy and a sense of community where each person recognises another in accepting each other's diversity and there is also a feeling of togetherness and of unity in creation universal values

Society is in existence because human beings have desires and needs. That can only be satisfied by cooperation. There is a need for community. No individual can live in isolation. Human life is entirely social. Community with justice is one of the foundations of democracy, every culture.

The stoics admitted the existence of a natural or moral law that gave certain minimum rights to all and only men without distinctions. "Government has to recognize such rights." Cicero, the orator, said: "no state except one in which people have supreme power provides a house for freedom." The emperor Justinian in the 6th century collected one code, "the Digest," which became the basis of civil justice in the western world and the forerunner of the Universal Declaration of Human Rights of the United Nations. It brought a new concept of freedom within the laws, equality in the common origin of men; brotherhood on the basis of one heavenly Father and enabled Roman laws to provide an early universal declaration of human rights.

Laws must be made only by the will of the people. King John of England in 15th June 1215 signed the "Magna Carta" which stated that:

-    The power of a ruler is limited

-    Human rights are more important than the

     sovereignty of the kings

After the "Magma Carta," democracy did not advance in England because a feudal class tried to undermine the right of the people. That has become the common problem in Third World countries after the advent of political independence. Leaders were confused between the power of the people, which they were supposed to respect, and their own personal will as an exercise in poor judgement over the people. In 1888, William of Orange from Holland was invited to England to replace James II and to rule according to a revised bill of Human Rights which secured the supremacy of the parliament.

In the United States of America, Thomas Jefferson drafted the Declaration of Independence, wherein he inscribed democratic ideals which had been brought to America from Europe and which excluded African American slaves and ignored women. In the Declaration of Independence we find the basic fundamental principle of democracy:

a. Men are endowed by God with the rights of "life, liberty and happiness"

b. All Government depends on the consent of the governed.

c. It's the right duty of people to unseat any government whose abuses and usurpations lead to nepotism.

d. The power of the government is divided into three sections: executive, legislative, and judicial.

The French Revolution was bloody. The king and hundreds of the nobility and the clergy were killed. Religion was set aside and the principles of morality changed. The concept of freedom and brotherhood was made known to every citizen.

In other nations, Kings were forced to accept reforms based on the principle that people are the source of authority. Kings had either to agree to rule in accordance with the constitution made by parliament or to abdicate.

Today the mentality of democracy has spread all over the world; the human rights declaration is humankind's most eloquent expression of opposition against tyranny and in support of the expression of the individual. To build up a political and social environment where the state and authorities are servants of the individual, and where respect for rights and duties of human persons is supreme is the aim of democracy.

Think of the terms Demos, like the people, and Cratos as the power of the government. "Democracy is known as the government of the people, by the people, and for the people" (Abraham Lincoln). Democracy is a way of ruling or governing the people. This ruling is usually done by a parliament. The ruling of parliament by representatives of the people freely elected by the people themselves is based on the principle of "One man, one vote." The representatives in parliament must stand for "the people."(or, until recently, men of a certain class and background)

The people must have the right to express their own opinions about the duties and sacrifices imposed upon them; they have the right not to be forced to obey without being heard and accorded full respect for their own dignity and freedom. This is based on the following principles:

- The freedom of religion and of conscience

- The freedom of teaching

- The freedom of speech and of press

- The freedom of association,

Those are freedoms of humanity

Freedom is a living thing. Good societies give the greatest freedom to their people; freedom defined not negatively, and defensively but positively as the opportunity to realise greater human values, genuine respect of the person. In our individual dimension, freedom is our capacity to direct our own development; the capacity to mould ourselves, it involves the acceptance of realities, basic realities such as the need for rest and food or as ultimate as death, not by blind necessity, but by choice. The acceptance of limitations can and should be a constructive act of freedom. The human who is devoted to freedom does not waste time fighting reality.

Freedom is the power to mould and create ourselves, the capacity to become what we are truly are. . When the structure fails through dictatorship, permissiveness of persons who deny this freedom to other persons, chaos, lawless, stagnation, immobilisation result and replace community and justice.

82

Democracy is a living and working system of government as such; it is never complex or fixed. No democratic system in the world today is altogether pure. Democracy must provide. Then, a permanent possibility of change.

In the religious-moralistic point of view, we find 3 ideas of democracy, which are:

a) The Christian idea of democracy (out of date)

b) The secular idea of democracy

c) The atheist idea of democracy

1. The Christian idea of democracy or George W. Bush's kind of democracy

The Christian idea of democracy tends to give the state a Christian background and this system does not always exclude other religions if the citizens want to follow them. Rulers believe in God and in the Divinity of Jesus and rule according to natural laws of the gospel; God is the author of the society and he made society to help men reach heaven. Man has an eternal end as well as an earthly end, for happiness. The rulers have received their authority from the people: "The voice of the people is the voice of God." Laws of God and Christianity limit freedom. Equality is in the rights and also in the duties. We are brothers because we are the sons and daughters of God. We do not find any laws against natural laws, for example non-legislation of divorce or birth control as they are against natural laws; politics will not be independent from morality; morality is considered here as the soul of society and secret of welfare.

2. Secular democracy. Example: Norsk Demokrati (Norway)

Secular democracy gives an artless background to the state and freedom of religion. The laws of the state prevail over religious laws because the different churches are looked upon as particular societies within the state, like any trade union. Leaders rule according to the laws of the state, without any religious influence. For the sake of a common welfare, the citizens obey the rulers. They do not see themselves as brothers because they have no common Father. They are equal before the laws and the laws limit freedom. Those laws are not against the laws of Christianity but offend what are considered natural laws in Christianity and in a moralistic point of view such as the law of divorce, or of birth control. Morality is kept out of politics. What is good for the interest of state is considered a right.

3. Atheist democracy

The system called Communism is not really democratic because the dictatorship has its own way of ruling, always monolithic or one party. The foundations of democracy - freedom of speech, religion, of thought, conscience - are often not always, totally forbidden and repressed, a mock democracy. The ruler leads the people not for their good but for the good and progress of the dominant ideology (the party or power of the country). The chief of the state is the supreme authority. They are brother/sister without a common father, their leader is their father. Only the ideology is free, so free that people could be sacrificed for its good.

In Africa, democracy is presented as just another form of totalitarian power because of its cultural background, but wherever there is human nature, there is the possibility of democratic form of government. In Africa years ago the chiefs were not only the makers of the laws and administrators, but were also judges of those who broke the law. We should consider historical facts in Africa to settle democracy. "There is nothing more difficult to plan, more doubtful of success, no more dangerous to manage than the creation of a new system" (Niccolo Machiavely 1513). It will be unwise to destroy the old system before building a new one.

Democracy must have limits. Democracy without restrictions is the worst form of government. Democracy includes taking the participation of all. Building a space of Dialogue. Laws are a necessary condition for democracy and any law is a restriction of our freedom. Democracy must be for the good of all classes of people. Political parties should work for the good of the society and not for the good of the parties themselves.

To build a dignified society we have to educate the public to be people because the masses, the mob or the public is the mortal enemy of democracy. Democracy is not about the number but the consciousness of the individual as being a part in the progress of the society. Therefore, *people* does not mean a mass of individuals, a crowd; *people* means citizens living together who are consciously responsible and aware of their duties, their rights, and their freedom is limited by the respect, the dignity and freedom of others. Democracy cannot be a government of the masses, for the masses, by the masses. That is why many countries have fallen into a cycle of crisis, because the people were not mature enough to settle on a power which would provide equality and freedom. The men of the future have to work through others and for others. A mass, a crowd, a mob lives and works by other peoples' convictions. A mob is always ready to follow a flag today or in the future. Being irresponsible for its actions provokes a dictatorship.

Training for democracy

Training for democracy consists of knowing and applying those fundamental rights as the rights for citizens to express opinion about duties or burdens that civil life imposes on them, the right not to be forced to obey in civil matters without first being heard, either directly or through representatives; this requires a sophisticated education and an understanding of the power of modern mass communication.

Mass communication: introduction

According to De Fleur and Ballrokeach (1989), communication enabled inventions and solutions to problems that marked the stages of human civilisation to be shared and passed down to succeeding generations. The stages in human communication are associated with development of speaking, writing, printing and the mass media in "the information society."Each development did not replace its precedent. Persons exist as units of the society. Alone, each person is isolated, meaningless; only when with communication with others does one become valuable. Different conflicts in our societies are misunderstandings or breakdowns in communication; we could eliminate those conflicts by applying the method of dialogue to human relations. When a person is engaged in communication, public relations (usually considered a form of lying), advocacy and counselling, one is a part of the society. Human life is essentially social and a democratic society must not be an individualistic society.

Personal opinion formation

The use of a basic education and personal development, the practice of social charity and social justice reducing selfish tendencies, useful meetings and well-prepared discussions, reading and talking and listening to one another requires wisdom and information. The interaction of people of different classes or denominations is useful for stability and an integrated society. The societies in the process of education and formation have to develop a sense of trust. Without trust, we are destined to endure at an increasing level of criminality as we see in most of the great capitalist towns of the world. Leaders have to be attached to principles and laws without discrimination.

Concept of freedom

A human being is free not because he/she does what she/he wants but because he/she does what is reasonable, and to go against the reason to do what he/she likes means that he/she is slave of his/her pride or of his/her instincts or something else. There is freedom when we follow the wish of the reason or of the soul unless these are reasonable.

When I am thirsty, I have the possibility to choose between water, cola or a beer. That is reasonable, but if I know that to drink too much beer will make me drunk, give me a headache or even waste my money, then choosing beer at that special moment will not be reasonable.

There is free action which is supported by awareness. I am not a slave; my instinct therefore is to follow feelings and wishes where they are against reason is slavery that will lead to irrationality

Human freedom, as we know, has limits, no one is fully free, all human power is totally restricted; we are born without our consent and we shall die without it. Nature itself limits our freedom; if you want to live you must breathe and eat. Can someone say I am free and so I want to live without breathing? The condition of our nature goes beyond our freedom. As our nature is limited, our freedom too is limited. If we could have an infinite, we could have an infinite freedom. If we are free, our neighbours are free too. We are not allowed to use our freedom to destroy the freedom of others.

A full understanding of democracy is based on a full understanding of freedom, equality and sisterhood/brotherhood of humans. Freedom is not rebellion but rebellion could be an interim toward freedom. Freedom means openness, a readiness to develop, to grow morally-spiritually-physically; it means being flexible; ready to change for the sake of human greater values.

From the universal declaration of human write, we can synthesise the following kinds of freedom:

Freedom of religion

Every person is free to choose his belief, or a faith, and the state has to make it comprehensible to the people to avoid tension and harm to the society. By respecting that freedom, we make ourselves ready for love and fraternity in the society because we will have tolerance to work with others. Religion is a personal affair and also a social affair. The 18th article of the Universal Declaration of Human Rights, approved by the U.N, says that every individual has the freedom of conscience, and religion and one of these freedoms includes the freedom of changing one's religion, and displaying one religion openly. This means not only personal worship, but social and public life within limits of laws.

By tolerance mentioned earlier, we have to understand firstly that men have to learn to develop a capacity of love instead of hatred or atrocities. Tolerance is one step to love. Tolerance does not mean love by any means. Love is a delight in the presence of other person's and affirming of their value, development as much as one's own. Love requires the ability to have empathy with another, to appreciate and affirm his potentialities; love also presupposes freedom. You can love someone as long as you are free. To love someone because, by accident of birth you happen to be a member of his family, is not love. Love is not a given by choice; you can love only in proportion to your capacity for independence, as Spinoza said: "truly loving God does not involve a demand for love in return." For example, to produce a piece of art requires that the artist be able to bring out his love, to give without thought of being rewarded. Then, to love means to give and to give demands a maturity of self-feeling.

Freedom of expression and press

Everyone possessing truth or constructive ideas has the right to pass it to others through speaking or other means of communications. Everybody has the right to express their opinions on certain facts and principles and to discuss the opinions of others. Those rights of speech and press are limited by the laws of justice, of charity, of truthfulness, of the church and laws of the state. A speaker or a writer can be a writer and may be prosecuted when using false statements as:

-       Defamatory libel,

-       Seditious libel which induces people in violence;

- Blasphemous libel against beliefs,

- Obscene libel,

- Official secrecy,

- Abuse of copyright,

- Contempt of court.

Freedom of association

Man is a social being; he is obliged to live in some association with other men. In a democratic country, citizens are allowed to have meetings and to join the associations they feel like joining.

All men are born free and equal in respect to their rights, meaning equal opportunities, equal justice and right. All men have the same type of soul, red blood, and flesh; they need air, food and drink; are born in the same way and will die in same way. As an Bantu proverb says, "All men's nostrils are directed downwards." Equality of men can be reached by education, public morality, honesty, fair standard of living, and democratic ways of living. As men are equal then they are brothers; there are no brothers without a common father. But by learning love, men can achieve true brotherhood. Lack of social charity makes a country unhappy. Citizens are often indifferent and that creates only anxiety, criminalities and other social evils. The Golden rule that we can find in all the big faith or religions in the world is: "Do unto others what you would like others to do to you," in other words "love your neighbour." You will learn to be a brother or to love someone by going to the other, by sharing feeling or interest, by sharing a common language. Interaction between nations, races, tribes, and classes should be made easy; international laws, institutions and laws must be strengthened. In general, for a world democracy we need a strong sense of internationalism and humanism.

Conclusion:

The new society must harmonize the basic values of the contemporary times. We must implement a democracy whose major institutions, resources, industry, health, etc., are public; a democratic world in which all states participate. And that can be accomplished by a total reform of education. An education through the art of human relations must stop inculcating the values of an industrialised society, such as materialism or endless competition, and promote values such as cooperation, charity, respect, peace, and consensus instead of majority rule. The world needs a democracy with converging ideas based on human rights, laws instead of diverging ideas like we have now, which create only conflict and confusion. A man's life must be based on cooperation with other men and the natural environment.

SUPPLEMENT 2

OVERVIEW ON AFRICAN THOUGHT

BY RAIS NEZA BONEZA

1. Definition of the terms

a. Philosophy in the strict sense

Philosophy is the study of thoughts, reasons in a systematic way by recording, writing sources or is a systematic way - for example Germans or Greeks philosophies.

For that matter African philosophy cannot be considered in a strict way or it was not philosophy in a strict sense. When in 1945, Placide Tempels published "The Bantu Philosophy", ed. Lovania, Elizabethville (Katanga, R.D. Congo), the dividing line between the philosophy of Africa and the African philosophy was going to be suppressed. It was around his work that a diversity of philosopher's thoughts and opinions raised; discussing and promoting the will of African people to emancipate.

b. Philosophy in general sense

Philosophy is a general life style like culture, songs, wise sayings, religions, or oral tradition. Therefore African philosophy existed in general sense because it was present in the concepts of their daily life.

c. African philosophy debate

Refer. Oruka, H.O.(ed), Sage philosophy : Indigenous Thinkers, debates on African philosophy, acts press Nairobi 1991

Question: Is there an African Philosopher? Yes or No

Many scholars have tried to ask questions as to whether, there is an African philosopher or not are what is referred to us as the African debate.

According to Richard A. Wrigth, the question is misleading; because it leads us to experiment and answer yes or no, just because of the grammar of this question. Richard is cautioning us to try to find out whether there is a specific body that can be justified as African philosopher. We should identify the answer no or yes as inadequate for a philosopher for it does not leave arena for further investigation.

We have told that philosophers in Ionian city, like Pythagoras, Tales visited Egypt for their information. Ionian philosopher contacts with others people stimulated that thinking in whatever Ionian, Egyptian thinking no one has been able to stress the origin of such thinking. There is like we can say a Dark story behind the history like the dark continent it self or the darkness on beginning of the creation from which come light. A History of Ancient western Philosophy, Applet on Century Crofts, Inc, New York, 1945, P.S.

Owens said Ionian's philosophers were influenced but did not say who influenced them. German philosopher Hegel constrained us to go back in history to see that Greeks received their foundation of knowledge from India, Africa, Syria and other parts of the world. Hegel immediately clamed that whatever Greeks received from Africa, Asia or Syria ; they obliterated it and made it their own. Hegel did not talk about African philosophy - he wanted that Greek philosophy to originate from Germany.

Prof E. Possoz of Brussels, in his book Bantu Philosophy, has made the following important observation ; up to the present, Ethnographers have denied all abstract thought to tribal people (Africans). The civilised Christian people were exalted, the savage and primitive man was denigrated and defamed. Out of this concept the theory of colonisation was brought.

We have forgotten that the Body in the centre of the Christians believe that Jesus Christ went back in Egypt (Africa) where probably he was taught by wise men. As Cheik Anta Diop said, Christianity is an African concept, it reminds us of Osiris who died and raised to save humankind.

2. The different trends in African philosophy

a. Ethno-philosophy

Ethno means particular group, tribe of people. Ethnology is a group of scientific studies of tribes or cultures. Ethno-philosophy refers basically to the study of group of people and their thoughts. Anthropologists, sociologists and philosophers all study ethnic groups of people in different fields.

In the writing of the tree groups of science one could find myths, folk-wisdom. And in such a writing one can see the wisdom of a particular group of people and one can see philosophy of a people in general sense.

Scholars who make a collection to discover and analyse these works are called ethno-philosophers. Their task is to enable description of a world outlook or thought system of a particular African community. Such scholars are Prof. Binti or Tempels as opposed to seeing Africa philosophy as a body of argued thoughts of a group of people, as in western philosophy. African philosophy is a communal thought and this gives it emotional appeal as one of its unique features.

Ethno-philosophy gets its material from Anthologists, Sociologists and Philosophers. And the sources are myth, folk-tales, folk-wisdom.

Myths are stories having some meaning, Folk-tales are traditional beliefs example : spirits, ancestors ; Folk-wisdom or wise sayings mainly from the elders.

Knowledge is facts not yet tested but wisdom is facts which have been tested on experience. The similarities between African traditional philosophy and western philosophy are that both philosophies deal with reasoning. Western philosophy deals with logical aspects while African philosophy is an experience.

b. The Sage Philosophy

The Sage Philosophy rejects the holistic remedy of African philosophy instead of seeking African philosophy by Folk-tales, folk-wisdom. This looks for Africab philosophy among the people – thoughts that are considered to be wise; it rejects western approaches and the ethno approach . The aim here is to show literally that it is not a necessary condition for philosophical reflection and exposition and that in Africa there are critical, independent thinkers who guide their thought and judgments by the power of reason and inborn insight rather than by the authority of communal consensus. This is to prove that in Africa there are men capable of critical and dialectical thinking without influence.

c. professional philosophy

In professional philosophy we have the work of many trained African philosophers who in general reject other trends of African philosophy. They take a general view of philosophy and argue that philosophy must have the same meaning in all cultures. The variation could be in emphasis that can be conditioned by culture or the background of the philosopher. According to this trend, African philosophy can only be by African philosophers.

3. The African's philosophy of universe

The African people observe the world around them, experience it and reflect on experiences. They observe things like the sky, stars, moon, sun etc. and also the earth in which they live and different manifestations of lives like river, lakes, mountain that make sense to them.

Alas I am talking about what we are losing, our conciliation with nature about what could be a benefit for the world around us in this new individualistic civilization where everything outside is considered to be a menace. At the end African will not have anything to present to the global world.

Africans have seen that limitation of Human in life and realised that life is short and the process of life at different stages too like circumcision, marriage, and death rituals...

All this experience calls upon a deep reflection about the course about life's facts in the Universe. There are numerous African ideas about the Universe that cannot be named at all. These views are presented in the form of myths, tales, symbols, legends and proverbs.

Africans think that the world is a created reality. Secondly, they believe the whole has a beginning somewhere and has been created by one great spirit (the Great Cosmic), man is the centre of the universe and above all other creatures.

There are two types of universe; the invisible and the visible. The invisible stands beyond the material world, represented as the sky or the heaven and the visible is the earth, material things alterable by times. The invisible is considered as the dwelling of Gods represented as the sun, the moon... and the visible as the home of creature and things like rock, mountains, men, animal...there is a link between the two universe and man is the centre of the two realities, from that appears the law of "causes and effects."

The universe as something eternal that it is endless both in space and time. The symbol of the universe is a circle or a snake. These forms depict the universe as a permanent reality. The Creator sustains the two parts. There is order and power in the universe, which is important in African world view so long as it is not disturbed. It can bring disasters; that to say that we are responsible for what could happen to us; what happens today is the response of actions we did before known in the esoteric as the "Karma law."

In our tradition, the order is subdivided in many levels. The law of nature, which is operating in the entire universe. It gives universe security and certainty and any change in the world leads to chaos. There is the moral order which operates among people. This moral order was given by God and angels or ancestors are in charge of the respect and application of those laws so that people live in

Harmony and peace. The aims of those moral laws are to safeguard the life of the individual and the community by knowing what is good or evil, right and wrong, truth and false, beautiful and ugly, and people's rights. Each society is able to formulate its values because there is moral order in the society. These values deal with relationships among people and between God, spirits, and men's relationships with nature.

In the African worldview, the universe is created by God. We consider even the law of the universe to be controlled by God, either directly or indirectly through his agents. Those agents are spirits and some people on earth. The relationships between Gods and his agents on earth have to be maintained. If that balance is not kept, it could lead to punishment and disasters. In African tradition, the balance can be kept through different taboos about foods, burial, shelter…Taboos were the meaning of keeping religious order between God and men.

There is a mystical power in the universe that could be found in the African medicines, practises of sorcery, magic, witchcrafts…there one will find mystical power that can be used for good and bad purposes. There are also Curses, which is used by elders or parents to find the culprits who have caused suffering to people by performing certain rituals. Among the Baluba, Lusanzu a murderer. Divination is another form of power that is usually used for good luck, prediction, and conversation with spirit.

The universe is illustrated by stories, myths; man is situated at the centre of the universe. And consequently, Africans always look for the usefulness of the universe to man and how man can benefit the universe. For this reason, man has divided things of the world into various groups for different purposes.

- physical needs: animals for feeding , building, medicine, fire, clothing, furniture
- religious needs: animals for sacrifices, rituals; Plants for worship and rituals.

Every existence in material form is possessed by some spirit and this it to prevent men from misuse of whatever man finds in the universe; for example, if you kill an animal unnecessarily, the spirit of the animal will haunt you down. Man therefore is the centre of the universe and he has to make proper use of things basically for physical needs, mystical needs and supernatural needs. Man is the beneficiary of the universe; when he disturbs the order within, he becomes the only victim of it. When he used it well he grows in his relationship with God, spirits and his fellow Humans, hence living in harmony in the universe

4. African cosmogony

The term cosmogony is used to designate the oral or written response on a pre-scientific and philosophical basis. Cosmogonists describe the form of myths, the creative action and primordial events to which the world holds its existence. In cosmogony, the creator (God) is represented as man (anthropomorphic form) and regarded as supernatural being. This creator carries out the act of creation by making use of other beings coming from himself, either through his creative will or by divine affiliation. He creates the universe either from nothing or from pre-existent-matter. He is the supreme artist.

According to the Egyptians, the universe was not created ex-nihilo on a particular day, but some matter existed before. This uncreated matter had no beginning or end. It was chaotic, matter without form. This chaotic matter was like non-being. Non-being does not mean nothingness (emptiness) but it is organised matter. This primordial matter is divine. Later, when philosophical thoughts developed in Egypt and even so in Greece, divinity became gradually replaced by principles or sources. Then primordial matter was believed to contain the law of its transformation. This is the principal of evolution of matter through the ages. This principal was also considered to be divine. In Egypt the word they use on this principal is "Kheper" it is the law of beginning, law of change, acting on matter through time actualising the archetypes. Beings were created in potency long before they were created in act.

Considering the movement of evolution, according to the African cosmogony, the eternal created matter passes from stages to another until it becomes conscious of itself. In this way the first consciousness springs up from "nous" in Egyptian thoughts. "Nous" in Greek word meaning God. In Egyptians'concept, it is Demiurge "Ra" who brings creation to completion.

Matter (eternal) ---- God-Ra ---- creature

The Egyptian cosmogony can be considered as materialistic because they granted that an eternal uncreated matter existed before the act of creation and evolution.

Chaotic matter + Ra = consciousness of things

It says Ra is composed of creation through word and at once the being comse into existence. Then there is a relationship between spirits and things that is an idealistic and spiritual worldview, no separation between spiritual and material. The real is necessary rational, since it is spirit and created by word. Hence the spirit can be external natures. "Ra" in Egypt or Imana in the Great lakes Region is the first God, the first demiurge of history who created through word. All the other gods of history came after him.

We cannot escape Egyptians when discussing African history, like Greek for western history. In Egyptian cosmogony, there is a historical link between the words of Ra, Ka, and all the universal reason present everywhere in the cosmos and everything.

"Ra" the first God, "Ka" rationality, spirit who is immortal principal and unites with the divine after death. Ka is given to what is created and when the creature dies, the Ka separates and goes back to the divinities.

In the work of Egyptian cosmogony, Ra created 4 divine couples:

- Geb and Nout unite with Ra to create earth and skies

- Shou and tetnout unite with Ra to creates air and space
- Osiris and Isis unite Ra who also unites with Ra to create human beings, Adam and Eve
- Seth and nethings unite with Ra to create Evil.

We can conclude that, with the conception of Ra, an idealistic or Spiritual element is introduced in Egyptian cosmogony with the appearance of the demiurge Ka. Later this idealistic influenced the Greek philosopher or became the basis of Greek idealism. Ra is the first God; he has neither father nor mother, and he is auto-genius, not engendered.

In black African cosmogony, the idea of "vital force" dominates thought. However, we can hear that the vital force can be found in person or spirits. This vital force is found in persons, Queens, spirits Kings, Chiefs, mysterious persons that continue the perpetuation of God work.

The Queen or King is believed to be continuing the work of creation through rituals, directives and rules of society. People believe in him and his rules because they see God in him, the King has to be strong since the vital force he has.

He might also be successful in his task; a   King wounded or sick had to leave the throne until he was cured. This was a sign of weakness. Through the death of such Kings, people say, he has hidden his hand here as a symbol and sign of power. For instance, among the Alur in the North-east of Congo, the death of the King cannot be announced until the successor is found. The word of a king is taken seriously because it full of vital force. The King has power even over life and death. He can for example curse one to death or bless one to continue to live among the Baluba or Bahema people in Congo.

a African concept of time

When something is done, time does not matter except as the execution of the function or duty. Time has very little influence on

African view. Time is only a composition of events which have either occurred or are occurring now or which occur in the near future. What has not taken place or what is not likely not going to take place soon falls in the category of "Non-time"? What are sure to occur are whatever falls within the rhythm of natural phenomena and this falls within the category of "Potential time." On the other hand, the "Actual time" is what is present and what is past. Africans look behind unlike western concept concentrates on the future. For example, a white man could ask you what your plans for the future. But an African will ask you what has already happened, who has died, funeral rites...for Africans, time moves backward.

Time reckoning is only for concrete, specific purposes in connection with events. It is nomathematical due to the fact that it is a composition of events. The relations with the event are considered as the relation to one another. In western society, time is utilised, sold and bought, but in our traditional life, time has to be created and produced, men do not have to be slave to it. In Buisha (East D.R.Congo) society, they counted time in term of rainy and dry seasons, cockcrows, birds, movement of stars and winds.

Bangala people in the centre of Africa have words to explain the future and the present; the words are Sika-oyo and Kala in Lingala, meaning present and past. Sika-oyo (Sikoyo) has the sense of immediacy, nearness or the now period of immediate concern for people since that is what concerns their presents existence here and now. Sika-oyo is also understood as a period in which people are conscious of their existence and within which they project themselves both into the short future and mainly in the past. For this reason the older the person is, the longer in in the Sika-oyo period. The community has its Siko-oyo period, which is greater that of the individual.

Kala overlaps the period of Sika-oyo, has its past before and events classified which events are actualised in the Sika-oyo dimension before moving in the Kala-wana. It has periods of achievement where everything finds its end point.

Every ethnical African group has it history, which moves backwards from Sika-oyo to Kala. There is no concept of the world moving forward towards the end of the world. With the events of death, the person continues to live in the Sika-oyo period but only in memory of relatives; he is dead physically but alive in memories of those who new him or her. The main entrance into Kala is reached when a person has survived from death or completely dead without any ashes of remembrance in the memory of anybody. This brings to mind the religious importance of marriage and it ensures one's existence even after death. One who has no children simply dies and is forgotten, but he who has survived continues to live in this survivors; the survivors and the deceased continue to relate.

To remove African from their ancestral land is what is often not accepted, people who leave their land voluntarily because of different necessities often visit their ancestral land for important rituals like birth, burial and other funeral ceremonies or marriage.

b. The Supreme Being according to Africans

The concept of being is strengthened by the belief in of a vital force which makes up the essence of beings. The Supreme Being is considered God the creator, this concept of a Supreme Being exists in all tribes in Africa. God is a part of the African View. That God of African is the same God that Christianity teaches about. He is known by different names. Often Africans identify the Supreme Being with his work. The Supreme Being has the following attributes:

- Omniscient: God knows all things, but in many African cultures, African religion is silent about knowledge of God, although there is no evidence pointing out that the Knowledge of God is limited.
- Omnipresent: God is present everywhere and we cannot escape his presence because is everywhere.
- Omnipotent: God is almighty, He is able to accomplish all things,

102

and men can need his help in their daily life. Nothing is impossible for him and if He does not answer the request of man, it does not mean that he is unable but for his will.

- Transcendent: God is beyond man's being; he is highly exalted above human's creation; he is without limitation; he is mysterious to human.
- Immanent: people can also approach him in prayers when the need arises. We are able to reach him.
- Everlasting: no beginning or end with no relation with time.
- Spirit: God has no body; he is invisible for our physical eyes.
- God is kind, merciful and good. This is manifested in the gift of rain, animals, children, victory, long life, and healing.
- God is holiness: in Africa. It is seen as sacredness; people during worship or other rituals imitate the holiness of God, even in gestures or dances organised in a systematic way.

- God is unique: no one can equal God; no one can be compared to him. His ways are different from human's ways.

The Supreme Being is seen as:

- Creator: he created the world
- Protector: people believe that God protects his creation and guides them.
- Ruler: he continues to rule his creation, he is the supreme ruler over the earth and he is known as the Supreme King, the Judge, Lord.
- Others functions like the giver, the healer come to complete his Greatness.

The African people pray during ceremonies for different stages in a person's life like death, puberty, death, marriage, birth, and harvest limitation. At the shrines, people offer sacrifices and prayers for different reasons resumed by wish for example for the restoration of health, prayer for the entrance in a new house, success or failure before and war, prayer before the journey. Most prayers are accomplished with a sacrifice. They are formal when those prayers are led by a religious leader or an elder of the clan and informal when led by the head of the family.

c. Notion of Divinities

People believe in various forms of spirits that form together with the Supreme Being to make the spiritual world. Other divinities are living dead and various spirits considered as monsters.

Most African society believed that the divinities do exist; they are part of the created universe, and the Supreme Being in form of spirit creates them. They are either created as such or they were once human beings who later on became deified. Some of the spirits exist as national heroes who have became elevated and became divinised.

We can explore the followings example:

Ashanti in the South of Ghana belong to the group of "Akan." They have a pantheon of divinities known as "Abosom" According to them, the Supreme Being created these divinities known as "Abosom" to accomplish its will by punishing, and serves as is spokesmen in this world.
The Yoruba of Nigeria; they have numerous divinities known as "Orisa." They are believed to have the largest number of divinities. The Yoruba divinities are associated with natural phenomena and objects. They are worshiped daily in Temples built by they devotes.
Ewe, living in Togo, have divinities known as "Mawu-lisa" Mawu-lisa are twins. Mawu represented by moon incarnates the feminine side and Lisa, the male represented by the Sun.
Karimojong in Uganda, they have "Ngipian"divinity which is the oversee of society.

There are numberless divinities in each tribe of Africa that reflect the spirituality of its people.

In some societies, the divinities carry out responsibilities for the Supreme Being through the ancestors to theirs gods.

Supreme Being ------ Divinities ------ ancestors ------ People

For example:

The Dinka in south Sudan: Nhialo---Yeeth---Atyep---People
Banyarwanda in Rwanda: Himana---Mizimu---Abachekuru---Abaturage
Bangala in R.D.Congo: Nzambe---Molimo---Bakoko---Bato

d. The Spirits

It takes about five generations for one to be completely forgotten by descendants. Then to be remembered as an ancestor one must be a parent (kinship) and also exemplary person. One must have a King, chief and a hero. There must be a blood relationship for one to be an ancestor.
Other spirits are just there in the world of spirits without any significant role. These can be the spirits of those young who died young without getting married. Such spirits don't become ancestors, but certain of them are turned into Ghosts especially of those persons who used to be criminals, evil, unhappy, buried in a foreign land. They are believed to wander in rivers and mountains and people cause them harm.

The spirits that were not human before are found in the environment and are associated with the force of nature. Among the Luo in Uganda, there is a river spirits known as Jokkulo. Women do not go to fetch water there late in evening because that is the time the river spirit comes out. The spirit could causes miscarriage for pregnant woman, sickness or sterility.

It believed that some spirits wandering could cause harm to people. Then there are various means like traditional medicines used to protect the people from bad spirits. Some means of protection are:

- Amulets
- Blessing of homes by the witch doctors

105

- Planting of a particular tree
- Small cuts on bodies
- Smearing of the body with special medicinal oil

e. The notion of Human

In Africa particularly there are many stories according to tribes and races:

- Human created from the skies (Lugbara; North east of R.D.Congo): the first man was from the skies, created by God. Lowered down to inhabit the earth. This thought is common among the people of the Nile Valley, Tanzania, Kenya. In Tanzania they say after been created in the skies, man was lowered down by spider thread. This tribe respect spider very much.

- Human created from the ground or earth: most Africa myths speak of God as a potter who moulded man on earth. However there are many versions according to regions. The Shilhuk of Sudan say that god used clay, which was of different colours to create men.
- Human being's creation of from water: others say human beings were created in water of marshes after being brought out of water and put on dry land. This myth is found from Akamba of Kenya and Nuer of Sudan.
- Human being's creation from a tree: some African people think that the first human fell off from the tree; this myth is found among Herero from Namibia and some tribes off R.D.Congo like the Mangbetu. The tree from which he fell off is called the tree of life. Among the Nuer, they consider that the first human fell of a Toumarine tree.
- Humans created in a calabash: among the Azande in R.D.Congo they believe that God created the first human being and placed him a vessel but later the vessel burst open. Because of that the Shagge call "God who bursts out humans."
- Human's origin from a hole: Akamba think that the first human comes out from a hole. From the hole, God brought man to live on the earth.

The basis of all these stories and others all over Africa is that humans originated from a supreme being "God." Man and woman both come from God either direct or indirectly. And they come in the completion of God's creation.

5. Inter-exchanges between Africans and western thinkers

Ionian thinkers visited Egypt. In Egyptian Cosmogony, the concept of being and matter of the origin of universe was studied before Plato and Aristotle. The being is composed of :

- The Zed or Khet, and this decomposed after death, soul and body compose being.
- The Ba that is the corporate soul or making to be recognised.
- Every being has a shadow.
- Every being has got the Ka that is immortal principle, which after death is united to divinity.

In the Bantu philosophy (tempels) there is a concept of :

- Mu-ntu which is existent with intelligence (Human) ;
- Kintu which exist without intelligence e.g. rock a or things.
- Han-tu localising existence e.g. spaces or place
- Ku-untu model of existence (manner of being)

There were no ethnologists, anthropologists or historians specifically for Africa. Those who studied Africa, did it in the favour of their own people. Historians produce books like Europe to learn about Africa, portraying Africa as a dark continent and so nothing good could come from it. Prof. Groves, the author of the « Planting Christianity in Africa » says it is a paradox that this vast continent while sharing in the earliest mysteries of Human race it was not yet opened up until the 19th century. Quoted in Black Men of Life, African heritage series, New York, 1970

For various reasons the western scholars did not credit the African people with simple fact like cultural tradition or forms of government. But they sought always to under look the Africans as not being human and hence to enslave them and exploit them.

Historians linked the North of the Sahara to European civilisation and the south of the Sahara as not, so that the South of the Sahara may remain a land of colonisation, exploitation and slavery. Studies have been taken and fossils found in the South of Africa and proofs have been advanced that those were African skeletons, but some western Anthropologists have rejected this discovery.

While western philosophy is academic, abstract and often dehumanised; the African philosophy is concrete and humanized. Western philosophy seems to separate thought from life. Or it tends to pretend that human beings are separated from their thoughts.

The case of individualism in western philosophy has overshadowed the peoples existence. Kierkegaard says Abstract speculation is the Cartesian and Hegelian manner has led to unspeakable impoverishment of life. Human existence, while particles of the universal idea, is not itself an idea or a purely ideal existence. Therefore abstract thought is an idea without a thinker. Concrete thought is from a thought that is related to a thinker. Because this abstract thought is associated with people like Descartes or Hegel; the African philosophy was not considered because it was concrete associated with life. Kant had argued that the Original Human species was white, appearing as dark brown only a result of oppressive climatic conditions, whilst Hegel wrote similarly that the characteristics that the feature of the Negroes is that their consciousness has not yet reached an awareness of any substantial objectivity. In Africa, life was not a manifestation of dialectical reason but, as Hegel put it, a succession of contingent happenings and surprises.

Since Hegel's exclusion of Africans history, anthropologists and others have stressed that because the reasoning capacity of all humans is the same, it is sociological rather than the epistemological differences in societies that are important.

6. Political nationalistic philosophy or contemporary African philosophy it's a philosophy of moderns time when some African leaders came up with their own thoughts in governing the people: for example Ujaama of Mwalimu Julius Nyerere (Tanzania), Harambe of Jomo Kenyatta (Kenya), Black-consciousness of Steve Biko (South Africa), African Humanism of Kaunda (Zambia), Negritude of Leopold Sedar Senghor (Senegal), Nyaho of Harap Moi (Kenya), authenticity of Mobutu Seseko kuku Gbendu wa Zabanga (R.Democratic of Congo).

All their philosophy is built on unity or communality. Political nationalistic philosophy was born during the political struggle of independence. It is a philosophy brought by African leaders. They tried to bring a new Africa political theory based on traditional Africa socialism and famillyhood. They argued that a true meaning of freedom must be accompanied by a true mental liberation and a return, whenever possible and desirable, to a genuine and authentic traditional African Humanism.

1. Nyerere Julius of Tanzania and Ujaama

Ujama is a Swahili word meaning Familyhood, Unity, and Togetherness. According to him the word was special reasons:

- it is African word a and so emphasised the Africans of the policies we intended to follow.
- Its literal meaning is familyhood so that it brings to the minds of our own and so that it brings to the minds of our own people the idea of mutual investment in the family.

Cfr: Nyerere , J.K, freedom and socialism Uhuru na Ujaame, Oxford University press, Dar-es-Slaam.1968.

2. Harambe of Jomo Kenyatta (Kamua)

Harambe is a political philosophy born in the 1950s by Jomo Kenyatta. who was a freedom fighter in Kenya. Kenyatta found a philosophy that called for the collective effort in the struggle of life. Harambe literally means pulling together, struggling together. If we successfully meet the challenges of life, we need to pull out together (Harambe). The community helps the individuals ensure health and the individuals also help in supporting the community in running these institutions. Harambe thought teaches unity, co-operation development and nationalism, which has, worked very much in Kenya.

3. Nyayo philosophy of Daniel Arap Moi

Soon after taking over from the Late President Kenyatta in 1978, Moi introduced a new philosophy, which he called Nyayo philosophy. Nyayo is a short name but in full that is Futa-Nyayo in Swahili, meaning "follow my footsteps." Follow in the spirit of our ancestors; in that way he managed to bring African people together for development and welfare of the people.

4. Black consciousness philosophy of Steve Biko

Steve Biko wrote a book "Black Consciousness and the Question for a True Humanity" article edited by Mothabi in Mokgeth, Essays On Black Theology, Johannesburg,1972. Page 21.

The African philosophy known as Black consciousness was born in 1969 in South Africa. It started within Christian Communities and as a movement of South African students Organisation known as S.A.S.O. The purpose of this movement was the liberation of people in South Africa then under the Apartheid System. It was so great that Africans were thinking that it was an evil to be black. So Black Consciousness was to wake up Africans to fight for their rights as Africans and Human beings.

In brief, Black Consciousness philosophy is an attitude of mind and a new way of life. It was a rebirth of a new black subject from the field of rejection to be fully human in life. It rejects the value system of the whites that devalues dehumanised Africans as useless. It liberates Africans from Negro-phobia; it liberate whites

110

from false ideas of about Africans and enlightens the Africans to fight for their equal rights and freedom.

The distinctive feature in the thoughts of all the contemporary African philosophers is that they developed a way of thinking charactised by protestation in quest of freedom and authentic identity as the Late president Mobutu introduced in the Democratic Republic of Congo (then Zaire) the philosophy of authenticity, which was another hidden side of the Negritude of A.Cesaire which called for the return to the source of African culture and moral. But after others, like Senegalese poet and philosopher the late President Leopold Sedar Senghor, it sustains conventional western thoughts. Senghor takes negritude into the political domain following the Second World War, with his famous saying, "Emotion is black as much as Reason is Greek." For Senghor, the African is characterised by the emotional faculty, devaluated in racist eyes but for him, another way of knowing the essence of things. For example water purifies, not washes, or fire destroys, not heat, the sun blesses us every morning, the heaven fertilizes the earth through rain.

7. Conclusion: Ubuntu in dialogue with humanity

Ubuntu is an African philosophy of humanism and co-existence. Ubuntu through umuntu ngumuntu ngabantu translates as: "To be human is to affirm one's humanity by recognising the humanity of others in its infinite variety of content and form" or "A human being is a human being through (the otherness of) other human beings" (Van der Merwe, 1996:1— italics mine)

For Africans and humans of all colors, and cultures, Ubuntu dictates that, if we were to be human, we need to recognize the originality in the diversity of our fellow human beings. That is, we need to acknowledge the diversity of languages, histories, values and customs, all of which constitute Africa and the world.

The Ubuntu philosophy emphasis on respect for particularity is vital for the survival of contemporary Africa. It contradicts the

Cartesian conception of individuality in terms of which the individual or self can be conceived without thereby necessarily conceiving the other. The Cartesian individual exists prior to, or separately and independently from the rest of the community or society. The rest of society is nothing but an extra added to a pre-existent and self-sufficient being.

Au contrair, Ubuntu defines the individual in terms of his/her relationship with others. According to this definition, individuals only exist in their relationships with others, and as these relationships change, so do the characters of the individuals. It represents a way of life based upon self-respect and respect for others as human beings, the latter becoming the source for finding one's own humanity. Ubuntu therefore implies knowledge and understanding of the people within a specific society. Originating in the African extended family, Ubuntu not only calls for respect for the mothers and fathers within society, but also for the elders, for they have the wisdom that accrues with age. Respect for siblings is extended to include an entire peer group, who should be treated like brothers and sisters. Kindness must be shown to strangers, for Ubuntu grants dignity to all people, a dignity born of mutual respect among human beings.

Ubuntu is especially appealed to when it comes to the settlement of seemingly unsolvable conflicts and insurmountable contradictions, especially in Africa and why not in the Middle East. ubuntu can be effective, in the first place because it is appreciated as an African thing, but in the second place and especially because, despite its globally-derived format, it introduces non-global, particularistic. Ubuntu is in favor of:

* Effectively managing   differences
* Dialogue
* Reconstruction
* restoration
* Forgiveness
* reconciliation
* Empowers people

* Positive Peace

The Ubuntu ethic of caring and sharing is not uniquely African. After all, the values which Ubuntu seeks to promote, can also be traced in various Euro-Americo-asian philosophies. That shows its universal and humanistic values that all nations and people could rely on in building Peace.

REFERENCES

----, "African traditional values for human development," in Agbasiere J.T., & Zabajungu B.K., eds., Church contribution to integral development, Eldoret, 1989, 45-62.

Caeneghem R. van, Het Godsbegrip bij de Baluba, Bruxelles, 1952.

-----, La Notion de Dieu chez les Baluba du Kasai, Bruxelles, 1956.

Calame-Griaule G., Ethnologie et Langage, La Parole chez les Dogon, Paris, 1965.

----, ed., Le thème de l'arbre dans les contes africaines, Paris, 1969.

Callaway C., The Religious System of the Amazulu, London, 1870.

----, "Divining by Familiar Spirits Among the Amazulu," in William A. L., & Evon Z. V., (eds.) Reader in Comparative Religion, New York, 1965, 340-344.

Pre-colonial Africa, Lawrence Hill book1987

Conflict transformation by peaceful means, (transcend manual) transcend.org

Peace by Peaceful means, Johang Galtung sage 1996

Pedagogy of hope, Paulo Freire1995

Disarming: Discourse on Violence and peace; Magnus Haavelsrud, arena 1993

Ethnic and National Identity In Africa Lessons & Resources on Africa, by Jeff Blair, North west School 1998.

Research in African literatures, volumes 33, number 4

Zimbabwe war of liberation: Chimurwenga War of the Zimbabwe National Union.

ZANU and the use of similar forces in Mozambique's RENAMO war against FELIMO.

UGANDA: The Long Road Home, Save the Children Norway, Save the Children Denmark, Kampala/Gulu. Søren Pedersen and Richard Young [2001].

Aderibigbe G., "Yoruba cosmology as a theory of creation: limits and assets," Asia Journal of Theology 13 (1999), 328-338.

Adelowo E.D., "A comparative study of creation stories in Yoruba religion, Islam and Judaeo-Christianity," African Theological

Journal 15 (1986), 29-53.

----, "A Comparative Look at Some of the Contents of Yoruba Oral Traditions, the Bible and the Qur'an" Asia Journal of Theology 1 (1987), 334-354.

Capron J., "Univers religieux et cohesion interne dans les communautés villageoises Bwa traditionnelles," in Fortes M., and Dieterlen G., (eds.): African Systems of Thought, Oxford, 1965, 291-313.

Casalis E., Les Bassoutos, Paris, 1933.

Chegwe A.O., "Re-Incarnation: A Socio-Religious Phenomenon among the Ibo- Speaking Riverines of the Lower Niger", Cahier des Religions Africaines, 1973, 113-135.

Chima A., "Dialogue with Traditional Religions in Malawi," Bulletin of the Pontifical Council for Interreligious Dialogue 28-29 (1975), 122-131.

Chinchen Del., "The art of hospitality African style," Evangelical Missions Quarterly 36 (2000), 472-481.

Chitando E., IAfrican Christian scholars and the study of African traditional religions: a re-evaluation," Religion 30 (2000), 391-397

Aderibigbe G., "Yoruba cosmology as a theory of creation: limits and assets," Asia Journal of Theology 13 (1999), 328-338.

Adelowo E.D., "A comparative study of creation stories in Yoruba religion, Islam and Judaeo-Christianity," African Theological Journal 15 (1986), 29-53.

----, "A Comparative Look at Some of the Contents of Yoruba Oral Traditions, the Bible and the Qur'an" Asia Journal of Theology 1 (1987), 334-354.

----, "African traditional values for human development," in Agbasiere J.T., & Zabajungu B.K., eds., Church contribution to integral development, Eldoret, 1989, 45-62.

Caeneghem R. van, Het Godsbegrip bij de Baluba, Bruxelles, 1952.

-----, La Notion de Dieu chez les Baluba du Kasai, Bruxelles, 1956.

Calame-Griaule G., Ethnologie et Langage, La Parole chez les Dogon, Paris, 1965.

----, ed., Le thème de l'arbre dans les contes africaines, Paris, 1969.

Callaway C., The Religious System of the Amazulu, London, 1870.

----, "Divining by Familiar Spirits Among the Amazulu," in William

A. L., & Evon Z. V., (eds.) Reader in Comparative Religion, New York, 1965, 340-344.

Capron J., "Univers religieux et cohesion interne dans les communautés villageoises Bwa traditionnelles," in Fortes M., and Dieterlen G., (eds.): African Systems of Thought, Oxford, 1965, 291-313.

Casalis E., Les Bassoutos, Paris, 1933.

Chegwe A.O., "Re-Incarnation: A Socio-Religious Phenomenon among the Ibo- Speaking

Riverines of the Lower Niger", Cahier des Religions Africaines, 1973, 113-135.

Chidester D., Religions of South Africa, London, 1992.

Chima A., "Dialogue with Traditional Religions in Malawi," Bulletin of the Pontifical Council for Interreligious Dialogue 28-29 (1975), 122-131.

Chinchen Del., "The art of hospitality African style," Evangelical Missions Quarterly 36 (2000), 472-481.

Chitando E., IAfrican Christian scholars and the study of African traditional religions: a re-evaluation," Religion 30 (2000), 391-397

Aderibigbe G., "Yoruba cosmology as a theory of creation: limits and assets," Asia Journal of Theology 13 (1999), 328-338.

Adelowo E.D., "A comparative study of creation stories in Yoruba religion, Islam and Judaeo-Christianity," African Theological Journal 15 (1986), 29-53.

----, "A Comparative Look at Some of the Contents of Yoruba Oral Traditions, the Bible and the Qur'an" Asia Journal of Theology 1 (1987), 334-354.

----, "African traditional values for human development," in Agbasiere J.T., & Zabajungu B.K., eds., Church contribution to integral development, Eldoret, 1989, 45-62.

Caeneghem R. van, Het Godsbegrip bij de Baluba, Bruxelles, 1952.

-----, La Notion de Dieu chez les Baluba du Kasai, Bruxelles, 1956.

Calame-Griaule G., Ethnologie et Langage, La Parole chez les Dogon, Paris, 1965.

----, ed., Le thème de l'arbre dans les contes africaines, Paris, 1969.

Callaway C., The Religious System of the Amazulu, London, 1870.

----, "Divining by Familiar Spirits Among the Amazulu," in William

A. L., & Evon Z. V., (eds.) Reader in Comparative Religion, New York, 1965, 340-344.

Capron J., "Univers religieux et cohesion interne dans les communautés villageoises Bwa traditionnelles," in Fortes M., and Dieterlen G., (eds.): African Systems of Thought, Oxford, 1965, 291-313.

Casalis E., Les Bassoutos, Paris, 1933.

Chegwe A.O., "Re-Incarnation: A Socio-Religious Phenomenon among the Ibo- Speaking Riverines of the Lower Niger", Cahier des Religions Africaines, 1973, 113-135.

Chidester D., Religions of South Africa, London, 1992.

Chima A., "Dialogue with Traditional Religions in Malawi," Bulletin of the Pontifical Council for Interreligious Dialogue 28-29 (1975), 122-131.

Chinchen Del., "The art of hospitality African style," Evangelical Missions Quarterly 36 (2000), 472-481.

Chitando E., IAfrican Christian scholars and the study of African traditional religions: a re-evaluation," Religion 30 (2000), 391-397

E.F. Schumacher, 1977, A Guide for the Perplexed, Abacus, London.

Myth or reality, Cheik Anta Diop, 1983 Lawrence Hill book

Pre-colonial Africa, Lawrence Hill book1987

Conflict transformation by peaceful means, (transcend manual) transcend.org

Peace by Peaceful means, Johang Galtung sage 1996

Pedagogy of hope, Paulo Freire1995

Disarming: Discourse on Violence and peace; Magnus Haavelsrud, arena 1993

Ethnic and National Identity In Africa Lessons & Resources on Africa, by Jeff Blair, North west School 1998.

Frymer-Kensky, Tikva. In the Wake of the Goddesses: Women, Culture and the Biblical Transformation of Pagan Myth. New York: Fawcett Columbine, 1992

Black Koltuv, Barbara, Ph.D. 'The Book of Lilith'. Maine: Samuel Wieser Inc., 1986.

Farrar, Janet and Stewart. 'The Witches' Goddess'. Washington, USA: Phoenix Publishing, 1987

Mary Daly, Beyond God the Father, Beacon Press (1985).

Pamela Eakins, Priestess: Woman as Sacred Celebrant, Samuel Weiser

Inc.

Riane Eisler, The Chalice and the Blade, Harper & Row, San Francisco (1987).

Riane Eisler, Sacred Pleasure.

Cynthia Eller, Living in the Lap of the Goddess: The Feminist Spirituality Movement in America.

Clarissa Pinkola Estes, Women Who Run With the Wolves: Myths and Stories of the Wild Women Archetype, Ballantine Books, New York (1992).

Elizabeth Schussler Fiorenza, Bread Not Stone: The Challenge of Feminist Biblical Interpretation, Beacon Press, Boston (1984).

Virginia Ann Froehle, Called into her Presence: Praying with Feminine Images of God, Amistad Press Inc.

China Galland, Longing for Darkness: Tara and the Black Madonna, Viking, New York (1990

The Black Pharoahs (Egypt's Nubian Rulers), Robert G. Morkot, Rubicon Press, 2000;

The African Origin of Civilization (Myth or Reality), Cheikh Anta Diop, Lawrence Hill Books, 1974

Somé, Malidoma Patrice, The Healing Wisdom of Africa: Finding Life Purpose Through Nature, Ritual and Commuinity, Tarcher / Putnam, 1998. An excellent description of the relationship of the Dagara People (West Africa) with This World and the Other World and a thorough comparison with Dagara culture and Western culture.

Tempels, P., Bantu Philosophy. Presence Africaine, 1959.

Williams, Geoffrey, African Designs. Dover, 1971.

The Image of the Black in Western Art, Volume One: From the Pharaohs

to the Fall of the Roman Empire

by Frank M. Snowden Jr

Willett, Frank, African Art: An Introduction. Oxford Univ., 197

Celenko, Theodore. Egypt in Africa; Indiana University Press; 1996

Davidson, Basil. Africa in History (New York: Macmillam Publishing Company, 1974)

Davidson, Basil. The Lost Cities of Africa, Little Brown & Co; Revised edition 1959.

Lan, D. Guns and Rain: Guerrillas and Spirit Mediums in Zimbabwe. London: James Clarrey, 1985

Parrinder, G., Religion In Africa. Penguin, 1969. Somé, Malidoma Patrice, Of Water and the Spirit, Tarcher / Putnam, 1994.

Somé, Malidoma Patrice, The Healing Wisdom of Africa: Finding Life Purpose Through Nature, Ritual and Commuinity, Tarcher / Putnam, 1998. An excellent description of the relationship of the Dagara People (West Africa) with This World and the Other World and a thorough comparison with Dagara culture and Western culture.

Tempels, P., Bantu Philosophy. Presence Africaine, 1959.

Williams, Geoffrey, African Designs. Dover, 1971.

Willett, Frank, African Art: An Introduction. Oxford Univ., 197

Leslau, Wolf, (ed.), Falasha Anthology. Yale University Press, 1951.

Tadesse Tamrat, Church and State in Ethiopia: 1270-1527. 1972.

Awoonor, Kofi Nyidevu, The Breast of the Earth. Anchor, 1975.

Balandier, G., Ambiguous Africa. Meridian, 1966.

Balandier & Jacques P. Maquet, Dictionary of Black African Civilization. Leon Amiel, 1974.

Bohannan, Paul and Philip Curtin, Africa and Africans. Natural History. Press, 1964. Duley, Margot & Edwards, Mary, (ed.) The Cross-Cultural Study of Women. Eliot, E. & Fagg, William, The Sculpture of Africa. Praeger, 1958.

Graham, Ronnie, The Da Capo Guide to Contemporary African Music. Da Capo Pr, 1988.

Maier, Karl, Into the House of the Ancestors: Inside the New Africa. New York: John Wiley & Sons, January 1998.

Maquet, Jacques, Africanity. Oxford, 1972.

Mbiti, John, African Religions and Philosophy. Anchor, 1970.

Murray, Jocelyn, (ed.) Cultural Atlas of Africa. Equinox, 1982. Paulme, D., Women of Tropical Africa. Univ. of Calif., 1960.

Parrinder, G., Religion In Africa. Penguin, 1969. Somé, Malidoma Patrice, Of Water and the Spirit, Tarcher / Putnam, 1994.

Somé, Malidoma Patrice, The Healing Wisdom of Africa: Finding Life Purpose Through Nature, Ritual and Commuinity, Tarcher / Putnam, 1998. An excellent description of the relati Bloch, Marianne N, Beoku-Betts, Josephine A. and Tabachnick, B. Robert, (editors) Women and Education in Sub-Saharan Africa: Power, Opportunity, and Constraints. Lynne Rienner Pub, 1998onship of the Dagara People (West Africa) with This World and the Other World and a thorough comparison with Dagara culture and Western culture.

Tempels, P., Bantu Philosophy. Presence Africaine, 1959.

Williams, Geoffrey, African Designs. Dover, 1971.

Willett, Frank, African Art: An Introduction. Oxford Univ., 1971.

Broodryk, Johann. 1995. Is Ubuntuism unique?, pp.31-37 in J.G. Malherbe (Ed.), Decolonizing the mind. Pretoria: Research Unit for African Philosophy, UNISA.

Broodryk, Johann. 1997a. Ubuntu management and motivation. Johannesburg: Gauteng Department of Welfare/Pretoria: Ubuntu School of Philosophy.

Broodryk, Johann. 1997b. Ubuntuism as a doctrine for the ordering of society. Unpublished doctoral dissertation, UNISA, Pretoria, South Africa.

Busia, A. 1967. Africa in search of democracy. London: Collins Press.

Degenaar, Johan. 1996. The collapse of unity, pp.5-27 in C W du Tiot (Ed.), New modes of thinking on the eve of a new century: South African perspectives. Pretoria: UNISA.

Khoza, R. 1994. African humanism. Ekhaya Promotions: Diepkloof Extension SA.

Koka, Kgalushi K. 1996. Ubuntu: a peoples' humanness. Midrand: The Afrikan Study Programme/Pretoria: Ubuntu School of Philosophy.

Koka, Kgalushi K. 1997. The Afrikan Renaissance. Midrand: The Afrikan Study Programme/Pretoria: Ubuntu School of Philosophy.

Lenaka, J. 1995. Some misconceptions about cultural differences: Intercultural Communication. Pretoria: Ubuntu School of Philosophy.

Louw, Dirk J. 1995. Decolonization as postmodernization, pp.67-73 in J.G. Malherbe (Ed.), Decolonizing the mind. Pretoria: Research Unit for African Philosophy, UNISA.

Lukhele, A.K. 1990. Stokvels in South Africa. Johannesburg: Amagi Books.

Macquarrie, John. 1972. Existentialism. London: Penguin Books.

11 See Islam et islamismes au sud du Sahara, éd. Karthala et Iremam, 1998

12. described by Johan Galtung in part IV of Peace by Peaceful Means

13. Idiamin Dada 1925-2003, Uganda president in 1962

1. 10 H. Meyer, 1984, pp. 15, 23, 24., H. Meyer, 1984, p. 15, H. Meyer, 1984, pp.16-22. H. Meyer, 1984, pp.23, 24, 26.

14 Nduguism derived from Swahili meaning comrade, brother, or relative

2 Preface by Léopold Sédar Senghor, President of the Republic of Senegal, to I'S. P. O." book one the International New Economic Order, 17 July 1980

P.S. See supplement World Citizens Democracy. (at the end, the essay supplement on democracy has been added as a rappel to the meaning of democracy)

Printed in the United States
41520LVS00005B/170

9 781593 440985